sex
money
&
power

*Smart Ways to Resolve
Money Conflicts and Keep
Them from Sabotaging
Your Closest Relationships*

Linda Barbanel, MSW, CSW

Macmillan • USA

International Standard Book Number: 0–02–861120–9

Library of Congress Cataloging Card Number: 96–068554

98 97 96   9 8 7 6 5 4 3 2 1

Interpretation of the printing code: the rightmost number of the first series of numbers is the year of the book's printing; the rightmost numbers of the second series of numbers is the number of the book's printing. For example, a printing code of 96-1 shows that the first printing occurred in 1996.

Printed in the United States of America

Dedication

I dedicate this book to the more than a thousand writers who have interviewed me about the psychological aspects of money. Answering your questions has helped me think about many aspects of the topic, enabling me to express my ideas in this full-length format. I hope you'll keep calling me!

Thanks go to my friend, Michael, who likes to be called "Swifty." Your support and humor during this project kept me going and laughing all the way.

Special thanks to my editor, Debra Englander, who worked with me in the past and gave me this opportunity to share my expertise with you.

Contents

Part III: **Money and the Opposite Sex**

Part V: **The Power Brokers**

Foreword

Every aspect of life has a money angle to it, and I feel like I've been asked to comment on them all. How and why we spend, save, donate, and invest is as interesting as what makes us gamble, shoplift, go into debt, and worry about money. Just what makes people buy from the "shopping channel," how friends can maintain a relationship when incomes are widely disparate, or how couples can create and maintain a financial partnership are all popular subjects. I hope that the issues that concern you most are addressed in this book.

Since 1983, I've been frequently invited to appear on radio and television programs, and I've been quoted in over a thousand publications on some aspect of "The Psychology of Money." The media cannot get enough information about such topics as money styles, allowances for children, fights over money, and dealing with cheapskates and spendthrifts. I hope I've made people aware of the reasons and dangers inherent in "compulsive shopping," and if I've been helpful in steering people away from money traps, I'm particularly gratified.

Money plays a significant role in all of our relationships, whether it's teaching kids about money, hammering out prenuptial or divorce agreements, asking for a raise, applying for a loan, helping parents plan for their retirement, or negotiating with shopkeepers, real estate agents, or anyone else—your success comes with knowing your own feelings, preferences, and limits. I hope this book will encourage you to make positive steps and take good care of yourself in all of your dealings with the important people in your life.

It's a fact of life that your personality affects your behavior. How you cope with dates, mates, kids, friends, parents, and professionals regarding money depends on such things as your gender, your earliest influences, and which qualities were nurtured in you and which were not. This book will help you relive your financial past so you can reevaluate what you learned about money. You can save the best and throw out the rest.

It's been said that people write about what they need to know more about. That is certainly true in my case. I come from a background where it wasn't nice to talk about money, and I didn't know much about managing it until I became an adult. If I could buy real estate, negotiate a mortgage, have my own investments, get my own credit, keep good records, be the executrix of my father's estate, and get my bills paid on time, so can you. It scared me to do these things, but it was more frightening to think of what might happen to me if I didn't take charge. Now I'm not afraid, and you won't be either. Keep in mind that when you set a challenge and meet it, your self-esteem grows and you'll feel terrific.

As a psychotherapist, I aim to help my patients become emotionally and financially independent. This book combines psychological understanding with practical help so you, too, can feel more capable of handling yourself in all of your relationships where money is a factor.

In researching the historical, social, and political issues that influence women's behavior with money, I became particularly excited. Now is the first time in all of history that many women are earning good money, managing it themselves, and taking the time and energy to make plans for their own future. The old taboos about discussing money are falling apart as women talk with each other about everything financial. Educated women are helping less fortunate ones get cooperative businesses going so they can learn skills and earn enough money to get out of bad marriages, off of welfare, and out of shelters for battered women. And, just think, if women would earmark their charitable contributions for these and other women's projects, how much more power could be unleashed.

While I've discussed security, power, love, and independence from a psychological point of view, I want to emphasize that truly feeling secure, empowered, loved, and independent comes from within, not from money. Money can help, but it's really *you* that has to take care of gratifying these needs for yourself. Such things as taking risks, meeting challenges, overcoming resistances, and then, finally, congratulating yourself will enrich you for the long haul.

Here's to sex, money, and power in your life!

Introduction: What We Talk About When We Talk About Money

What would you do if you won the lottery?

I ask this question during my talks and counseling sessions as a way to warm people up because so many of us are uncomfortable talking about money. This question usually elicits some pretty conservative answers—at least initially. I remember speaking to one woman (let's call her Andrea) and getting a particularly sedate, low-key response: "Sock it away in the bank, I guess." I reminded her of my profession. I'm a psychotherapist, and that means that I love hearing about other people's fantasies. I asked Andrea to open up just a little more about the dreams she might be able to fulfill if she hit it big financially.

"I'd go for a trip," she answered.

"Where?" I asked.

"Europe."

"Really? How long would you stay?"

"Oh, I don't know. A couple of weeks, probably. The main thing I'd do with the cash is pay off the bills and invest it sensibly."

"That's pretty basic, Andrea." I said, smiling. "Let's think about it this way. You didn't just win any lottery. You won the super-lottery—not some two-bit, million-dollar-a-year affair, mind you, but the *big* money. You're in Bill Gates' territory now, because you hit the once-in-a-decade jackpot. What on earth are you going to do with all that cash?"

Andrea laughed. I could sense that she was beginning to think bigger about her wildest dreams.

"Hmm. Let's see." Andrea smiled. "Well, I'd start off with a round-the-world trip. First Europe. Then Africa. Then South America. I've always wanted to see Rio de Janeiro."

"Around the world. Okay. Just once?"

"Yes," she said, "But that would only be the beginning. I'm going first-class. I'll do some traveling around the States, too. Visit a couple of old boyfriends who broke up with me. Show off the Mercedes. You know."

"So you're going to be taking a lot of time off from work."

"Work? What's that?" she asked. "I forgot to tell you, the morning after I heard about my big win on the news, I walked into my boss's office and told her to go jump in the lake. Then I hired away all the staff and started up a competing firm, one that I check in on about once or twice a year. It makes a lot of money, but its principal goal is to give my old boss a pain in the neck. The fact that it's hugely profitable is just a nice bonus."

Clearly, Andrea was getting the idea behind my fantasy game.

"Where are you going to live?" I asked.

"Well, I'd buy a new house," Andrea answered thoughtfully. "I mean, you did say I was in Bill Gates' league, right?"

"Right."

Like many women, Andrea focused on simple changes. She could see herself traveling around the world—once—and she would get a new house. However, she was still having a hard time thinking *big*. She could afford to buy several lavish houses but, as with some women, she has relatively modest expectations. I had to encourage her to broaden and lengthen her outlook. Slowly, she was able to contemplate buying a swanky condo in New York and an apartment in Paris. Considering investments, charitable contributions, and new activities for having fun didn't come easily to Andrea, as they don't for many women.

For most of you, the idea of having a lot of money is certainly appealing. But why? There are dozens of possible reasons, and the fantasy game is a great way to isolate some of them. The answers people come up with during this game often shed surprising insights into their deeper motivations and attitudes about money and earning a living.

"If I Won the Lottery, I'd . . . "

Here are some common answers to the question of what you'd do if you won the lottery. What would you do?

- Quit my job.

- Make sure I was completely secure and protected from the kinds of financial risks my parents faced. I'm not going to let what happened to them happen to me.

- Get my kids through college and make sure they have an easier time of it than I did. If they make out better than I do, then maybe some of the things I went through will have been worth it.

- Make some donations or contributions to a charity so I could make a difference in the world.

- Help out some close friends who have been there for me in the past.

When you hear about the potential disadvantages of winning the lottery or having a great deal of money, you may find yourself chuckling in disbelief. While you may be thinking, "Yeah, right, I could handle whatever problems money brings," you should ask yourself these questions:

- Would living with your children be easier or more difficult if you were phenomenally wealthy?

- How many friends and relatives do you think would line up at your door asking for a piece of the prize?

- How would you go about selecting financial advisors you could trust?

- When you made new friends, how could you be sure of their real motivations in wanting to become part of your circle?

- How would you handle the financial disparities between you and other members of your extended family? Would sudden wealth make a difference in how your family related with you?

- Do you think some people might resent you?

- How would you feel about a heftier tax bracket?

- What kinds of changes would you expect in your friendships if you made a lot more money? Do you think you might talk and behave differently with your friends if you suddenly had less in common with them? What kinds of stresses will these relationships experience if you don't share the same tastes or budgets when it comes to entertainment, food, or leisure activities? Do you think you'd stay friends?

- Do most of your friends earn roughly the same salary as you do? How much time do you spend "talking shop" with friends? Would a radical change in your financial situation affect your everyday interactions with these people?

- Do you understand the tax implications of having large sums of money and are you ready to deal with the IRS?

There are advantages and disadvantages to having a great deal of money just as there are to having too little money. This is a world marked more often by shades of gray than by polar opposites. Although you are often tempted, consciously or unconsciously, to assume that you would be able to resolve your most important problems once and for all if you had all the money you could possibly want, the truth is that wealthy people are not, as a general rule, any happier than other people. Many, of course, are quite unhappy!

Let's Play Monopoly!

Do you remember playing Monopoly as a child? I've talked with hundreds of people in seminars and counseling settings over the years, and have only come across one person who had never played the game. It caught on, of course, during the Great Depression of the 1930s, a time when millions of people felt out of control of their financial situations. The game has shown remarkable staying power over the years because of the emotional needs it meets.

Do you remember what it felt like to win—or at least ride a winning streak—while playing Monopoly? It was pretty exhilarating, wasn't it? It felt great to accumulate all those little green houses and the larger red hotels. It felt great to charge exorbitant rent, and it felt great to pray that someone would land on your property so you could collect the tax . . .

Playing Monopoly lets you feel all sorts of things about money. The strongest feeling—the one that has stuck with us after all these years of playing Monopoly, has a name. It's called "greed," and it's something everyone experiences. Even though the money is fake, the emotions behind it are not.

Do you remember how it felt to lose at Monopoly? If you were losing, the game seemed endless. Did you ever have to stop and remind yourself that it was only a game? You'll no doubt recall feeling somewhat depressed, down, and defeated. Even funny money has the power to make us feel complacent, manipulative, and opportunistic. When the jig was finally up and you had to pass over your property to someone else, did you feel a certain inexplicable sense of personal failure?

What Would You Do with a $100 Bill?

Finally in a talk or session I'll show a real $100 bill. If I ask a person in the front row if it is indeed real, I'll sometimes get a response like, "It's been a long time since I saw one," or "I don't know, I never had one," or "You took a real chance carrying that around in New York City." Very few people know whose face is on the front, by the way. Those who are used to having these bills say they spend them too fast to study them much.

I then hand the bill to the closest person and ask her to come up with some thoughts and feelings about it before handing it along to the next person. For a little permission to divulge and share secrets, I remind them that psychotherapists are always interested in thoughts and feelings. After a few moments of silent contemplation, I ask for their reactions. Some people will minimize one hundred dollars by saying things like, "That will buy you one shoe on Madison Avenue." Others will maximize it and say that they wish they had a hundred dollars because they know how to stretch it to buy things for the whole family.

Money makes us think and behave in ways that go against our morals. It's OK to think about stealing, but money is not worth going to jail for, wouldn't you agree?

When I ask, "Who thought of stealing my one hundred dollar bill?" there are a lot of smiles, maybe guilty ones. Initially, no one admits to wanting it, but there's usually one courageous soul who eventually confesses. Yes, that's truly the one honest person in the room. Is there anyone who wouldn't pick up a loose bill on the sidewalk? How about a penny? Hove you accepted more change than you should have from the supermarket? Would you report an undercharge to your credit card company? Money can make you do things you wouldn't think possible, and it certainly can make you think of trying to get away with lots of schemes. How does a "get rich quick scheme" make you feel? You won't go to jail for your thoughts, but beware of actually putting one into action.

Getting money without earning it stirs up lots of peoples' juices. Is it worth going to jail for? Does the end justify the means? How does money affect your relationship?

Even play money has the potential to make us feel these intense emotions. It's not a crime to admit to similarly strong feelings of emotion when dealing with the real thing!

Money is one of the two or three most powerful motivating factors in our lives. Money stirs up our juices in a way that virtually nothing else does. Many of us have asked ourselves silent questions about money—questions that we may or may not choose to share with the rest of the world.

- Is there a way to get money without working for it?

- Does the end really justify the means?

- What would happen if I cheated just a little, just like other people are probably doing, where money is concerned? If they did notice, what would I do? If they didn't notice, how would I feel about myself?

- What do I have to do to get enough money?

What This Book Will Do for You

Money is, I believe, one of the last great taboos. There is still tremendous hesitation about discussing financial matters openly, even in a therapeutic setting. In therapy, I occasionally encounter people for whom money-related conflicts threaten to destroy relationships with family, friends, and colleagues. Some of these patterns are rooted in very early childhood experiences. In this book, you'll explore the early—and later—influences that often result in financial hang-ups with everyone from shopkeepers to spouses, kids to aging parents, friends to foes, colleagues to bosses. In this book, you'll learn some workable strategies for managing those hang-ups.

Is this book right for you? The answer is "yes" if you are willing to look at the patterns you may have developed for dealing with the people and the money in your life. Specifically, this book is meant to help you:

- Find out how your reactions to money may be affecting your relationships with others, and learn how to manage money-related conflicts and misunderstandings and communicate more effectively.

- Learn what you can—and can't—expect money to do for you.

- Take the first important steps toward gaining true control over your finances.

- Examine the thoughts, fantasies, and feelings you have associated with money over the years.

This book is different from most money books. It doesn't offer nuts-and-bolts advice on investments. Instead, it offers psychological insights into money behavior and explores practical suggestions for overcoming the fears that may be preventing you from being emotionally and financially independent.

In *Sex, Money and Power,* you'll look in detail at how money can affect your relationships with spouses, friends, parents, coworkers, and children, ex-spouses, and financial advisors. As you do so, you should take special note of the ways you can moderate your money strategies and improve your relationships. You'll learn how to encourage healthy relationship patterns. You'll learn how to deal with your own expectations and fantasies. You'll discover new, unexplored ways of doing things, and you'll find out about old ways you've picked up along the way.

Let's get started!

Money and You

Chapter 1

Out of the Cradle

*W*hen Erica was a little girl, she didn't have an allowance. She asked her mother for money from time to time, when there was a good reason to. The emotional atmosphere in her home, however, was such that she didn't like to ask, and so she didn't ask very often. That's not to say that she didn't want things. She simply got used to not having them.

"I remember going to Woolworth's with my mother," Erica told me, "and playing with some cheap toy there while my mother shopped. I must have been around six years old. I remember asking her to buy the toy for me—it wasn't an expensive one by any means—and I remember very clearly the way my mother told me that we wouldn't be buying it. I don't recall asking for another toy ever since that day. It's not that I never got toys for Christmas or birthdays. I just didn't ask for anything."

Once, Erica told me about the feelings she had in fifth grade when she couldn't make out the writing on the blackboard from where she was seated. "I prayed to God that I wouldn't need glasses. That was an expense." By this time, Erica had become a master at making do with what she had. She had one pair of dress shoes and one pair of school shoes, and they each lasted for quite a long time. Since she took good care of her clothes—many of them carefully preserved hand-me-downs—she hardly ever wore out anything. This is a trait that

Erica retains to this day. "I still have the black velveteen jumper I bought for a high school sorority dance," she boasts. "I've shortened it a few times—it's gone from calf-length to mini—but it's still hanging there in the closet."

Erica's parents lived through the Depression years, and that period had a profound influence on them. Money was for the necessities—and perhaps an occasional night out. "Restaurant dinners were a real treat when I was growing up, and I still feel that way about going out," Erica says. "I don't recall going to a sit-down restaurant until I was about nine, and at 21 years of age I was still unsure about which bread-plate was mine."

When it came to dealing with questions of finances, Erica's childhood memories are not pleasant ones. There was "a good deal of tension and yelling in the house," Erica recalls distinctly, when her father and his brother dealt with her grandfather's taxes. "My father just plain didn't spend money easily," she says. "Our home never got remodeled, as the others on the block did, and over a period of 20 years the furnishings changed once."

"Dad was a self-denier who would say 'no' to any expense," she continues. "I saw him as no fun. He never complained. He managed to make it through life with simple pleasures and no frills. He expected the same of the rest of the family, and I learned to adapt. I remember him going nuts once when I talked for more than three minutes on a long-distance telephone call. It was simply against his principles to pay for anything other than basic service and it hurt him to pay for more than the bare necessities."

Erica's mother was conservative and resourceful. She was good with her hands, so she made her own hats, handled routine maintenance around the house, and cut the grass and pulled the weeds in the lawn by herself. "As far as decorative touches went," Erica recalls, "at our house it was mainly Depression-era glass gifts, bric-a-brac my parents had gotten as wedding presents, or things my mother's friends gave her when they redecorated or when their parents moved or died."

The family was not poor. Erica's mother and father had simply learned to be extremely frugal during the early 1930s, a period when a good many people lost all faith in the country's banking system, stashed their money in hiding places in their houses, and took any job they could get in order to keep their families housed and fed. "Mom saved her money," Erica recalls. "She kept all of her old clothes and shoes in the attic. She always said she was saving the old clothes in case she needed something to wear. I guess I take the same approach with clothes. Actually, I'm like her in many ways. I'm good with my hands, and I like a large balance in my money market account. As for my Dad, well, I swore I'd never be like him. And I'm not . . . exactly. I don't deny myself, but I don't think I'm ever going to be a world-class spender. There's always this little voice in my head nagging at me, telling me to live within my means. Telling me to save. Telling me not to buy what I don't need."

Many factors—beliefs, attitudes, unspoken messages, important people—affect the way you think and behave about money. You might find that some of your earliest behavior patterns will continue throughout your life unless you take a look at them.

How are you like or unlike your parents when it comes to money, possessions, and spending? What values did you pick up from them? Were there financial quirks or messages that your parents passed along to you when you were young? Do these make sense for you now as an adult?

What you learned from your family in the past is often the basis of the conflicts you have with others about money today. The way finances were handled in your home when you were a child may have an immense effect on you as an adult, both with regard to your ability to talk about money in the first place, and your success in handling it.

To begin to understand how your family life affects your use of money, you need to think about how money was handled when you were growing up. To help, take the short test that follows. Mark your answers on a separate sheet of paper.

Family Money Style Quiz, Part One

1. Speaking very broadly, how much money did your parents have when you were a young child?

    a) We got by all right.

    b) Things were usually tight at the end of the month.

    c) There was plenty of money, usually more than enough.

2. Did your parents experience an unexpected financial reversal at any point in your childhood?

    a) Yes, but it didn't affect the emotional atmosphere in the house in any meaningful way.

    b) Yes, and it affected the emotional atmosphere in the house noticeably.

    c) No.

3. Which of the following statements best describes your parents' attitudes toward money? (Circle more than one if necessary.)

    a) "Money is a means to an end."

    b) "Money is the root of all evil."

    c) "Money is for necessities, but it's also for fun."

    d) "It's as easy to fall in love with a rich man as it is with a poor one."

    e) "Love conquers all."

4. Which of the following statements best describes your mother's role in dealing with household financial issues?

    a) She handled the household bills.

    b) When necessary, she pretended to know less than she did.

    c) She shopped till she dropped.

5. Which of the following statements best describes your father's role in dealing with household financial issues?

    a) He took charge of most aspects of the family finances.

    b) He was generally ineffective.

    c) He hit the roof from time to time.

6. Which of the following statements best describes the way you dealt with money and purchasing decisions while you were growing up?

    a) I had an allowance and how I spent it was pretty much up to me.

    b) I more or less got what I asked for.

    c) I had to try to convince my parents to buy me specific items, and I had varying degrees of success.

7. Which of the following problems do you recall your father and mother clashing over? (Circle as many as are appropriate.)

    a) Different spending priorities

    b) Excessive debt

    c) Late-payment issues

    d) I honestly don't recall my mother and father arguing about money.

8. Which of the following statements best summarizes your family's philosophy toward purchasing decisions?

    a) "You really ought to be happy with what you have. There are people who would be very envious of the way you live."

    b) "Keep up with the Joneses."

    c) "The best things in life are free."

(Answer question 9 only if your mother worked.)

9. Which of the following statements best summarizes your feelings at the time about your mother holding a job?

   a) Now everyone in the neighborhood knows that Dad's paycheck isn't big enough to support the whole family.

   b) Thank goodness for the extra money.

   c) I guess she's too busy to spend time with me.

   d) Why shouldn't she work if she wants to?

(Answer question 10 only if your mother worked.)

10. How did your father react to your mother having a job?

    a) It didn't affect him in any meaningful way.

    b) He was somewhat threatened, but he adjusted.

    c) He wanted her to stop working as soon as possible.

    d) He was glad to be off the hook financially.

Family Money Style Quiz, Part Two

Study your answers and see if they stimulate some memories or more questions. You might ask, for instance, "Why did my father always make me feel so guilty about asking for anything new?" Write down your own questions, but don't try to answer them right away.

Then take a look at the questions below.

If it seems likely to be helpful, relax, close your eyes, and remember what it was like to live in your home as a child. Remember how your body felt. Think about how you felt when you wanted something. Could you ask for it easily or did you hesitate? How did it feel when you wanted something expensive? If you prefer, you may simply free-associate on the topic and see what memories come back.

1. If financially oriented traumas were part of your childhood, what did you learn from them? How have they affected you in the long term?

2. How did your parents treat you when you asked for money? How did you feel when you were refused? What were your private thoughts about these events? Did you make any secret vow to do things differently when you grew up? If so, how have you fared?

3. What would you say is your biggest fear about money? Is it similar to a fear one or both of your parents had on this score?

4. If financial success was part of your background, what have you learned from that experience?

5. If financial need was part of your background, what have you learned from that experience?

6. Do you have a financial fantasy? Describe it in detail.

7. If you came into sudden wealth, what would you do differently than your parents?

What spoken or unspoken beliefs and attitudes from your early family life have affected your own decisions and predispositions when it comes to dealing with money?

Whether they knew it at the time or not, your parents encouraged certain traits when it came to dealing with money, and because you wanted your parents to love you, you identified with those traits and tried to mirror them. Changes are possible, of course, and individual personalities do have a way of affecting the way you deal with money issues. Generally, you tend to copy your parents' ways of doing things—including the way one or both handle money. Sometimes, though, you will behave in the opposite way. In turn, you will pass on to your children your attitudes and concerns about money.

Your parents' money values and quirks, whatever their origins, have an immense effect on your own outlook on financial matters. However, once you understand where your own predisposition comes from, you, as an adult, can choose whether to hold onto patterns that are unhealthy for you or change these patterns.

Even if you have repeated a pattern for years, you can modify it if you truly want to. By identifying these hidden values and unspoken beliefs, you'll make them easier to examine—and, if necessary, reject. By identifying the patterns that your parents passed along to you, you will be able to make conscious decisions about the way you want to think and behave with regard to money and your interactions with others about money will improve also.

By putting the words to the music of these hidden values and unspoken beliefs about money, you'll not only identify these patterns, but you'll be in a perfect position to take responsibility for them. You'll either decide to retain a particular style, or modify it. This means that with a little work you won't have to, or want to, blame others about your finances. Putting the words to the music comes first!

How do you start that process? Look through the notes you just made and the answers you just wrote down. Identify the patterns that seem most relevant. Put together a brief summary of your parents' money philosophy and how you think it has affected you, then—take a step back—and try to gain a little perspective.

If your parents were having troubles, emotionally or financially, during the early child-raising years, try to trace how their reactions played out with regard to your own money patterns. If you can remember how your parents reacted to the stresses they faced, you will gain some valuable insights into your own financial styles.

Think back to your childhood and whether your parents answered questions about money. Were you able to ask these questions freely? Also, did your parents respond differently to your concerns about money? If your mother and father confused you with their divergent money habits, what did you do?

What Other Factors Affected Your Early Money Training?

The spoken and unspoken attitudes your parents passed along about dealing with money are the most important factors that shape your own attitudes towards financial matters. They're not the only factors, however. Here are some other issues to consider.

The Earliest Influences

It's important you understand that it is hard to talk about money because your earliest influences happened before you had the ability to speak. As a Freudian, I believe that what you learn in the nursery and in your first five years of life establishes many of your behavior patterns for the future. Look at some key concepts:

- **Anxiety.** Nobody had a blissful childhood without some anxiety. That's why we all feel some insecurity. The more fearfulness and insecurity, the more some people save money to feel better. When babies are uncomfortable, they rely on adults to relieve whatever the problem is. If, for example, you were given a pacifier, or were fed as soon as you showed some signs of discomfort, as an adult, you may seek out similar instant gratification when things go wrong. If you're nervous or distressed, you may turn to food or shopping or other people as a way to relieve your anxiety. Obviously, if shopping is your preferred means of relief, there may be financial consequences. Those who have a low tolerance to anxiety may have high credit card debt. As we'll see later in the chapter on Love Buyers, some people have to shop to get relief from such feelings as anxiety, and it's very expensive. Others pay bills ahead of time to ward off anxiety, or they'll save money for a rainy day, bargain hunt to stretch dollars, collect things of value that could appreciate, or have the self-control to pass up buying things.

  On the other hand, if your parents didn't immediately respond to your needs as a child, you may have felt hopeless in your attempt to get relief and give up trying. This may translate into a lack of ambition, or depression. You may feel unwilling to work hard, since rewards come late or not at all. To protect yourself and to feel a sense of control, you may minimize the importance of money. Recall how Erica reacted to her parents constantly saying no. Instead of learning to manage money realistically, she learned how to be frugal. Or, you may focus all your energies into work and making a good living as a way to provide your own gratification and be as independent as possible as we'll see in the chapter on the Freedom Searchers.

■ **Feeding Patterns.** Back in the 1940s, many parents believed that children should be fed on a rigid schedule, thinking it would build character. In fact, rather than learning patience, the hungry child usually grew angry at his or her parents. Some children who didn't get enough food grew into adults who wanted to buy everything. Others became obsessed with having enough money and, like squirrels, stashed away bits of money and lived as frugally as possible.

On the other hand, children who never have to signal their hunger may grow up expecting that everything they want will come their way and that they will never have to wait for anything.

■ **Toilet training.** Toilet training also may have a significant impact on your attitude toward money. After all, issues such as withholding obedience, dominance, submission, control, and rebelliousness all come from this period of your life. This is a time of power struggles. If, as a child, you didn't like being told what to do, you may now resent paying bills and taxes and wait until the deadline to take care of these responsibilities. You may be a procrastinator and do these things when you're good and ready to. You may be cheap with compliments, gifts, and feelings. Children trained too early may later throw up their hands at other things that seem to be "too much to handle." That's a common reaction of people who have trouble keeping records and taking care of financial matter.

Power seekers do to others what was done to them. They want to tell others what to do, and sometimes this is done in intimidating ways. Love Buyers, on the other hand, probably got a lot of attention and encouragement during the training period, so they continue to give money and other valuable things away to get more appreciation and love.

Other Members of the Family

Your parents almost certainly had an overriding influence on the way you formed your approach to money, but other members of your family may have played an important role, as well.

Draw a family tree that includes your grandparents, aunts, uncles, and cousins. Leave enough room to write some notes on your tree about how a particular relative thought about or handled money. Write down not only the person's name and the years when you were together, but also the kinds of influences that person faced. Note the personal and world events that shaped the way they looked at money. What part did wars or recessions play? Your parents' employment and career moves? The birth of your siblings? Moves?

If there was one family member who had a particularly strong influence on your money-management style—say, an uncle who ran a business and employed many members of your family—be sure to note that person's influence on your family tree.

Birth Order

Don't be surprised to learn that you and your siblings had "different parents"—at least when it comes to the financial patterns that you received. This is a very common experience and reflects changes in your family's dynamics over time.

If you're the oldest of two or more children, you may have been exposed to different financial circumstances and expectations than your siblings. Typically, first-time parents are a little anxious on both the financial and personal fronts. They're new at parenting, and they may have had to deal with the additional pressure of having recently separated, emotionally and financially, from their own parents. Careers are often less certain around the time of the birth of a first child than they are later, so that, too, may have had an influence on you.

POINTS TO THINK ABOUT IF YOU'RE THE FIRST-BORN CHILD

- If your parents moved out of a neighborhood in which one or both of them had spent a good deal of time, they may have had some pretty serious adjustments to make during your early years. Friends, family, and other support networks may have been few and far between, and this may have led to stresses, financial and otherwise, within the relationship.

- If you were the first child, and especially if you were the first grandchild, it's possible that you were showered with gifts and special attention, that more photographs were taken of you than of your siblings at the same age, and that other tokens of your status, material or not, were a critical part of your early upbringing. How did these events affect you?

■ Conversely, many first children report that they were treated to fewer privileges than their later siblings, as they had no one to "pave the way." Were you a guinea pig for your family as far as their parenting skills were concerned? Did your parents show a markedly more liberal approach to allowances, gifts, or presents with your siblings than they did with you during your early years? If so, how do you feel about this?

■ Regardless of your parents' emerging attitudes toward parenting and money, if you were the first-born child there's a very good chance that you were expected to assume a certain leadership role within the family at an early age such as taking care of younger siblings. How was your performance, or non-performance, of this role usually rewarded? How do you feel about assuming a "leadership role" now, especially with regard to financial matters?

POINTS TO THINK ABOUT FOR ONLY CHILDREN

If you're an only child, you probably carried all the burdens and privileges of first-borns—and you may have had the added challenge of developing your own system for managing cooperative and mutually satisfying endeavors, especially where material things were concerned. Most only children don't learn much about sharing because there are no siblings in their family.

■ If you didn't have to share as a child, you may not much like the idea of sharing as an adult. How has this factor affected your work and personal relationships? How has it affected the way you handle money?

■ If you were indulged as a child—and there's a good chance you were, since you had no one to compete with for financial rewards and parental attention—is it possible you continue to expect to be treated this way?

■ Even if you are not the first-born child, come from a very large family, and were born long after your next oldest sibling, it's quite possible that the first-born or only-child patterns just discussed may be worth reviewing. This "second generation" first-born pattern is quite common in large families.

POINTS TO THINK ABOUT FOR SECOND-BORN OR "MIDDLE" CHILDREN

In many families, the second child is born shortly after the first has been weaned and toilet trained. If this chronology applies to your situation, there's a good chance that your primary caretaker was spread fairly thin during your first year of life. Whoever had to take care of two babies at the same time was engaged in a very difficult undertaking, one that no doubt extended to all hours of the day and night, and made serious demands on even the most saintly patience levels.

■ The way you were played with, cared for, toilet trained, and generally interacted with may have been marked by pressure to quickly complete one stage and move on to another. It's possible that your parents rushed you into developing skills that you did not yet possess, such as drinking from a cup or dressing yourself. If you did not react well to these spoken or unspoken pressures to perform, you may be wary of challenges later in life. You may feel overwhelmed and not ready to deal with the financial realities of everyday life.

■ If you and your older sibling are close in age, it will probably be helpful to you to take a few minutes now to note whether and how the two of you differ in dealing with financial issues. There probably are marked differences, and this could be another way you and your siblings tried to individualize yourselves.

■ Can you take the time to talk to your parent(s) about how life changed for them when your sibling arrived? How established was your father in his job or career during your early years? Did having a larger family initiate a move to a larger home? How did that go? How did the family's financial routines change upon your arrival?

■ Ask yourself some questions, too. Were there issues of competitiveness, fairness, and differentiation to address? How has holding the second or middle position affected you emotionally and financially over the years?

The "youngest-child" pattern, one generally marked by a more laissez-faire attitude from parents, fewer parental expectations, and greater levels of nurturing and support, may also apply to a child who was thought to be the last child in the family, but who was joined by a younger sibling at a much later point.

Older siblings often complain that "the baby" in the family gets away with more than they ever did, and parents, whether they admit it openly or not, may just conclude that the older children have a point. There are a number of reasons for this pattern, one being simple fatigue.

POINTS TO THINK ABOUT FOR THE YOUNGEST OR "BABY" IN THE FAMILY

■ As the years pass and more children make demands on the family structure, parents not only have less time to poke into the affairs of the youngest child, they have less energy than they did a few years back. Parents may also make a point of indulging the youngest child in the family.

■ It's possible that you've become used to getting your way with others as a result of being the beneficiary of this "baby syndrome." How has this pattern affected your adult attitudes toward finances and, especially, material rewards? How has it affected your relationships with others?

■ There may have been less anxiety around the issue of child-rearing during your early years than your older sibling(s) faced. Your parents, after all, probably felt a little more confident approaching the job of raising you than they did the first time around. There also may have been a more established career path, and a greater sense of financial security, for your working parent(s) during the time that you grew up than during the time that your sibling(s) did.

Are there long-term or short-term issues of resentment between you and your siblings in connection with any of these issues?

Gender Issues in the Family and in Society

As many women have long suspected, there are often stark, gender-related differences in the direct and indirect ways parents teach their children about how to deal with money. As you'll see in the next chapter, many women come to the conclusion that they were raised in a way that discouraged them from assuming personal interest in, or responsibility for, their financial affairs, and that strong social pressures reinforced and amplified these early lessons.

Now that you have an idea of the other early factors that may have played important roles in shaping your emerging money awareness, it's time to look at the question of how your status as a girl, and later as a woman, shaped your outlook on financial issues. This question raises many important issues relating to social roles, personal responsibility, and how women handle their money. It is worth spending some time exploring such far-reaching topics. These issues are what you'll focus on in the next chapter.

Chapter 2

A Brief Historic Overview on Women and Money

*T*hroughout history, women have worked. Some of the earliest cave paintings show women making pottery. Women were also farmers and food preparers, and may have made the tools used in cooking. They created baskets and slings from grass to carry babies. However, these and other accomplishments of women were rarely acknowledged. Instead, the men are credited with creating fire, defeating enemies, and providing for the family. This lesser—some would say subservient—position for women persisted for many centuries. A woman's value was in her ability to bear children, not her ability to make economic contributions to society. An extreme example is that of fifth century Athens, where married women were kept locked at home, guarded by servants and dogs. They were not allowed to go to the marketplace alone, where they would see other men. By keeping their women virtually under house arrest, the Greek noblemen made sure that any male heir was their own son.

Despite the vast number of working women today, women have become integral members of the economic system only fairly recently. This explains why old attitudes persist and why women today are looking for guidance in relatively new territory. Women have been able to own property, attend universities, vote, work in traditionally male-dominated professions, and support themselves for perhaps two hundred years. For centuries, society expected women to stay home and let their husbands support them. Few women, except for prostitutes, worked for sufficient money to be able to support themselves. Only since the Industrial Revolution of the 18th century have women generally been paid relatively well for their work. Even in the 19th century, some women took to disguising their gender by using pen names (George Sands and the Brontë Sisters) in order to gain recognition for their work. In most current societies, women are able to work outside of the home, receive recognition, and get paid, even if that pay is not the same as what men get for the same job.

Key Influences on The Changing Identity of Women

- **World War II**   During this conflict, more women went into the labor force than ever before. With men serving in the armed forces, women were hired to perform the jobs previously held only by men. Women's social and political horizons were broadened. They could leave their homes and work in offices and factories. Society, at last, had to re-examine the woman's role.

- **Post-war era**   With men returning home and expecting to return to their jobs, women faced a return to their earlier roles. After all, the media message was that women should be mothers and house-wives while the men worked. Many women refused to step back into this role and continued to work, often at lower salaries than men and in worse conditions than men. However, for about a decade, many women did retreat back to their homes and didn't work.

- **Civil rights movement**   Landmark civil rights legislation ended discrimination not just for minorities but for women as well. Job opportunities opened up, albeit slowly, for both women and minorities.

■ **Feminist movement** Consciousness-raising sessions and the banding together through many liberation activities enhanced the power of women. Women fought and won abortion rights, equal opportunity, and affirmative-action programs.

■ **Birth control** Lowered birth rates gave women choices they previously never had. They could work or not, and marry or not. The money saved from having fewer children kept the economy going, too. Some women's shopping has contributed to the hyper-consumptive society, and in certain instances has made two pay-checks necessary to maintain this high standard of living.

Women in the 90s

The differences between today's mother and the stereotypical 50s TV mom who stayed at home with the kids are dramatic. Today women work, whether by choice or of necessity. In fact, the stay-at-home mothers and their bliss-ful ignorance of financial matters now seem almost ludicrous. With the divorce rate steadily increasing, many women end up as heads of house-holds, supporting themselves and their children, often with minimal help from their former husbands.

For some women, this independence and financial power is difficult to handle. They are trailblazers without a guide. After all, many of these women were raised in an era when women did stay home and relied on their hus-bands to support them. Now they don't have to stay in dead-end jobs or abusive relationships. Women need to examine their expectations of being cared for by their husbands as well as being treated all the times on dates. When women worked, their salaries were often small and therefore not considered significant contributions to the family finances but now women's paychecks are necessary. Decision-making has changed.

Today, as a result of educational opportunities and changing economies, women are a significant part of the economic—as well as social and political—culture. While some women, especially those who aren't in the workforce, may feel dependent on their husband for security, an ever-increasing num-ber of women are in the enviable position of being financially independent.

These women don't have to rely on their husbands or fathers for their well-being.

Along with financial independence comes responsibility. Women who are earning more money have the right to decide how to spend, invest, or save this money. The smart women are those who continue to develop as professionals so they will be able to advance in their careers. These savvy women also educate themselves about money so they're able to maintain their hard-won independence. Educational and financial institutions of the country have responded to this new market by holding "women's seminars" along with general ones designed to provide women with the skills needed to protect their financial independence for the future.

Conflicts over This New Identity

The road to financial independence for women has not always been smooth. While the feminist movement helped bring women together and provided the impetus for many women to improve their lives through education and employment, the path for other women was not always clear.

Some women could not (and still cannot) reconcile the image of an independent women with the more traditional "feminine" role. The successful working women with her conservative suit and briefcase combated her fears of aggressiveness and learned to be assertive and to be loved by men who earned less than they did. They had to prioritize their time so work didn't take the fun out of life. As the media picked up on this issue, countless magazine articles appeared about the new role of women and the super-women who did it all—juggling work, husband, children—except perhaps making time for themselves.

Even now with women succeeding in once male-dominated fields of science, law, and medicine, the conflict between women's independence and their relationship with men is never far from the surface. Consider the difference between advertisements in men's and women's magazines. Ads in women's publications are filled with products focusing on improving their attractiveness—clothing and cosmetics—while men's publications feature high performance computers and products such as electronic goods.

Makeup and Makeovers

It's not surprising that women's magazines feature so many cosmetics ads. After all, this is a billion-dollar business. Cosmetics address the secret concerns of so many women who want to look more attractive—younger, hipper, sexier—whatever is "right" at the moment. It is an expensive quick fix to feel better. It's important to observe that women will spend an extraordinary amount of money on "make-up" to compensate for what is missing in their lives. For many women, spending money on cosmetics means they're going to look better and be more attractive with the ultimate purpose of being loved. The money is spent to buy love. As you'll see from reading this book, this is only one example of how women use money to get love. Other women will take more drastic steps when they don't feel good inside. They will spend money on their outside. Look at how much is spent on plastic surgery, clothing, beauty parlor services, gyms, and spas.

Many of these women come to talk to me. And, in many cases, the women are spending this much time and effort to alter their appearance instead of focusing on other concerns related to their emotional well-being and "inner being." By talking about their needs, these women may learn to use other means to focus on what they're feeling and wanting, rather than spending money to improve their "exteriors." Psychotherapy has been an enormous influence on women to help with problems related to important attitudes, career, people, and stage-of-life issues.

Don't get me wrong—there's nothing terrible about wanting to look good or pamper yourself. Women need to express themselves and make demands about what they want, just as men have always done. But using money to avoid dealing with feelings and pressing issues isn't the answer. Keep this important message in mind as read this book and learn about the impact of money on your life and those of people around you.

Four Styles of Money and Spending

In the previous chapter, you looked at how events in your early upbringing may have shaped your attitudes toward money. In this chapter, you've learned about the changing financial roles women have. Now it's time to look at how these influences have affected your life.

I've identified four primary styles of approaching money and spending. These are four varied approaches to spending that apply to most people. As you begin to read about personal economic issues, you'll start to recognize these "types."

- For the group I call *Keepers,* money is something to hold on to in order to feel secure.

- For the group I call *Love Buyers,* money is often abused as a means to get love.

- For the group I call *Power Seekers,* money symbolizes control.

- For the group I call *Freedom Searchers,* money is a symbol of freedom and a reinforcement of feelings of self-reliance.

Each of these four styles is worth reviewing in detail since you, or someone you love, almost certainly operate from one or more of them when it comes to managing money and relationships. Very few of you, I've found, don't know *someone* who falls into one of the four groups. Some people have elements of more than one, but usually one prevails.

In the next chapter, we'll take a close look at the Keepers.

Part II

Understanding and Dealing with Your Money Personality

Chapter 3

The Keepers

The Super-Saver: Suzanne's Story

*S*uzanne could write a book called How to Squeeze a Dollar out of Every Dime, *except that she's too busy. She has proudly and passionately made a science out of spending as little and saving as much as possible. She devotes most of her energies to the fine art of squeezing the most she possibly can out of her husband's paycheck. She works on charitable activities as well, and as the vice-president of her local PTA, she passes on recipes for homemade Play-Doh to teachers. As treasurer of Friends of the Library, she's in charge of approving expenditures. Naturally, she approves very few.*

Suzanne clips coupons, changes banks when she notices an offer for free checking, and plans family vacations only after exhaustively researching all the various Bed and Breakfast packages available. She may well hold the Dallas/Fort Worth record for taking advantage of rebates.

Although Suzanne sometimes acts as if all the scrimping is a game, it's a game she seems unable to stop playing. She's accustomed to keeping a daily diary of her expenses; she categorizes these monthly so she knows where all the money goes. She'll check the financial page in the newspaper to see how the family investments are doing. As long as they're on the rise, she's fine, but if there's a down turn, she gets anxious and upset. If her husband forgets to tell her that he's made a cash

withdrawal with his ATM card, there's usually an argument. Actu-
ally, there are quite a few arguments in Suzanne's household.

The fights appear to be over money, at least on the surface. In fact,
they are, on a deeper level, about Suzanne's feelings of insecurity. If
she doesn't feel in control of the finances, her old worries from child-
hood, where both money and love were in short supply, bubble up.

Suzanne once provoked a nasty argument with her sister, Marie,
when she threw a plastic bag into the trash before it had been reused.
"To Suzanne, throwing out one plastic bag is a sin," says Marie. "It's
not because she is trying to be a one-woman conservation movement,
but because it means one less fraction of a penny in her account. I told
her that the Depression ended before she was born. Mom had reasons
to reuse paper bags and wrapping paper, but that plastic bag I threw
out wasn't going to make anyone go hungry. Mom kept on being care-
ful about waste after times got better, but I think Suzanne has out-
Mommed Mom."

Like many people who feel more secure when they save, Suzanne
takes heroic steps to make sure she'll have what she needs when she
needs it. It's good to have a plastic bag on hand for storing leftovers,
but is it worth a fight with her sister to have 47 instead of 48 of them?
Mom may have saved everything, Marie wonders, but does that mean
that the habit has to be passed down through the generations in
perpetuity?

Here, as happens in so many families, one child, Suzanne, has
repeated a parent's habit while the other offspring, Marie, avoids it.
Long ago, Suzanne learned that her best chance for winning a smile of
approval from her mother lay in imitating her. She did get some mea-
sure of love this way, and gradually, after repeating this behavior over
the years, the habit of extreme frugality became part of her personality.

Suzanne is a super-saver. From one perspective, she's a great credit
risk, a solid citizen, and an inspiration to the financially shortsighted
people who live from paycheck to paycheck and don't worry about
how they'll manage in the future. Some of her neighbors admire her
thrifty habits and saving skills.

However, while bankers and others may love ultraserious savers, family and friends may resent them. That's because people like Suzanne tend to provoke guilt on the part of those who splurge or even think about it. Their children may experience them as naysayers and cheapskates. Their spouses often feel shortchanged, both emotionally and financially. Frugality comes across, at times, as withholding and meanspiritedness.

As you can see, for a Keeper like Suzanne, money is something to hold onto, something to use to enhance feelings of safety and security. Of course, all of you find ways of linking money to security issues now and then. The rent does, as a general rule, have to be paid, and the kitchen is a nicer place to be in when it contains groceries. But for the Keeper, obtaining security through money is a pervasive pattern. Sometimes, the Keeper's concern with money borders on an obsessive pursuit.

Here are some questions to ask yourself about the way you deal with money; answer them honestly, and mark your responses on a separate piece of paper. By taking the test all the way through, you'll get an idea of the common traits of the members of this group.

The Keeper's Quiz

1. How many "bargain" items of clothing do you keep in your closet, even if you seldom or never wear them?

   a) None or one

   b) Two to four

   c) More than five

2. Which of the following statements best reflects the way you typically choose to deal with credit card bills?

   a) "How much is the minimum balance this month?"

   b) "Anyone who doesn't pay off the balance in full every month is paying too much interest."

c) "Credit cards are a huge temptation. I never, or hardly ever, use them, unless there's an emergency."

3. Someone tells you about an investment opportunity that offers you some very attractive terms . . . *if* you agree to tie up your money for at least five years. Which of the following statements would come closest to describing your reaction?

   a) "If I really trusted the broker, and had known him or her for some time, I'd consider investing as much as I could afford."

   b) "It might be worthwhile to invest a little bit of money in this arrangement."

   c) "I could never stand to have my money tied up for that long."

4. How do you pay for your vacations?

   a) Take a spontaneous approach and enjoy things as they come.

   b) Develop a budget and try to stick to it, but leave enough for unforeseen activities.

   c) Prepay for everything with package deals.

5. After balancing your checkbook, you realize that, for a day or so, you were operating under a false impression. It turns out that you made a huge arithmetic mistake on a recent deposit, and have a lot less money than you thought. Which of the following statements best reflects your reaction?

   a) "Oh well, I didn't lose anything because I never had it to begin with."

   b) "That could have been a real problem and I'd better keep it from happening again."

   c) "I could have bounced a major check; think what that would have done to my credit rating."

6. To what extent do you use coupons to save money at the supermarket?

   a) Almost never

   b) Occasionally

   c) Frequently

7. How often do you worry that you'll end up penniless in your old age?

   a) Almost never

   b) Once in a while

   c) Often

8. How frequently do you buy lottery tickets?

   a) Once a week or so, perhaps a little more sometimes

   b) Once in a while

   c) Never

9. Which of the following statements comes closest to describing your financial philosophy?

   a) Living well is the best revenge.

   b) Money helps, but it doesn't buy happiness.

   c) A penny saved is a penny earned.

10. How would you be most likely to describe the prospect of taking a trip to Las Vegas, for a weekend of recreational gambling with a group of friends?

   a) "It could be a lot of fun."

   b) "It's the kind of thing you have to be careful about, but if you set limits on the amount of money you're willing to risk, it could be a nice form of recreation."

   c) "That's a recipe for disaster. I could lose everything."

Scoring

Give yourself 1 point for every "a" answer, 3 points for every "b" answer, and 5 points for every "c" answer. Here's how to interpret your score:

36–50 points:	For you, money represents security.
26–35 points:	You keep money in perspective relatively well.
10–25 points:	You tend to indulge yourself.

If you scored high on this quiz, the need for security may be affecting the way you interact with people and money more than you realize. Money may have a way of dominating your relationships and behavior. In all likelihood, it represents safety to you. You may expend a great deal of effort to guard it and wring the most value possible out of it. If you're a Keeper, it's probably fair to say that, whether you are more used to dealing with large amounts of cash or small ones, you get pleasure out of the accumulation of money.

Keeping an Eye on the Bottom Line: "It Is Its Own Reward," Say the Keepers

Many Keepers were let down by people in their past; they often come to the spoken or unspoken conclusion that money is simply more reliable than people. It does, after all, always come through when it's needed—assuming it's been saved in the first place, of course. The sad irony is that, in their attempts to protect themselves emotionally with money, many Keepers find themselves living a life that is perpetually insecure.

If you scored very low on the quiz, you're almost certainly not a Keeper. You may even want to ask yourself whether you are sometimes putting yourself at greater risk than you should in your financial affairs. (See the section on Security Shunners later in this chapter.) If you scored in the medium range, congratulations, since you probably take a balanced approach to questions of risk and reward.

No matter how you scored on this test, please read this chapter in its entirety! If you are a Keeper, it will provide you with important insights on your relationship patterns. If you're not a Keeper, this chapter will be helpful to you as you deal with the Keepers in your life.

There are variations on the Keeper type:

The Money Martyr: Sandy's Story

Sandy is a widow in her mid-fifties whose brand of thriftiness might seem to make her a soul sister of Suzanne. There's an important difference, however.

Suzanne feels a sense of happiness and acceptance when she engages in hyper-frugality, Sandy is unhappy about anything related to money.

When a coworker who's just gotten a promotion says, "Let's celebrate," Sandy insists on going to a diner with an all-you-can-eat special. She has never been able to accept gifts graciously. If you give her a scarf, she'll tell you that she's still wearing the one you gave her last year. "How many scarves do I need?" she may ask. "I've only got one neck." Offer to shovel her sidewalk when she's hurt her back and you'll hear, "Thanks, but I'll do it slowly." Self-denial rules Sandy's personality and her lifestyle. What she doesn't need, and chooses not to indulge in, are major issues for her. It's as though she can't really approach interactions with others without somehow appealing to the idea of self-sacrifice on her part.

Sandy, who was the youngest of four children, lost her father when she was seven. Sandy's brothers took odd jobs and her sister took care of her while their mother typed up bills for the local grocer and cared for elderly people in the neighborhood. Most of Sandy's childhood memories are shadowed by the scarcity of money in her family. She learned not to ask for special things. When she did ask for something, her mother said she would have to help around the house first. As soon as she finished one chore, her mother gave her another to do, and then another, before coming through with the promised reward. Sandy resented this, but she never expressed her feelings about the cycle. Instead of talking back to or defying her mother, on whom she was completely dependent, Sandy learned to get by without the pretty things she desired. And, many times, she also didn't get the encouragement to try herself out with after-school activities or a camp experience. Sandy grew up learning how to make personal sacrifices. She also grew up chronically depressed.

During her 22-year marriage, Sandy occasionally worked part-time, but thought she could contribute best to the family budget by sacrificing when it came to her own needs. She did little to develop her own talents; after all, she wasn't shown how to when she was young. Even though her sketches showed talent, Sandy didn't go to art classes or any other afterschool activity. Although she could go to classes, museums, or galleries nowadays, she rarely does. She enjoys music, but she doesn't even take advantage of the free concerts in her community. Recently, she passed up two chances to spend a weekend away at a friend's cabin. Both times, she loaned her car to her married daughter instead.

It's hard for Sandy to spend money on herself. She'd prefer to have it available to give to her son for his condo. At times, she'll complain of feeling like a doormat, but she hasn't done much to change the situation.

While Sandy's life may sound miserable, it has a certain logical consistency. Sandy is a money martyr. Money martyrs act the way they do in order to protect themselves from envy. They don't want anyone to feel resentment toward them for having material things. What leads them to believe that others might feel this way? Deep down, that's how *they* felt at some point toward others for having things that they did not.

At some point in their lives, money martyrs felt deep envy about the material possessions of others, and concluded that feeling that way was either too dangerous or too uncomfortable, so they buried their emotions. Money martyrs expect that other people will be envious of any of their possessions. Since they usually lack a healthy foundation of self-esteem and self-approval, money martyrs feel they can't afford to be disliked. That's why they disclaim privilege and possession at every opportunity.

As a self-denier, Sandy hopes she'll get some recognition for giving of herself on such a regular basis. However, by denying her most important part—her Self—she became selfless, and that's too much to give. Unfortunately for people like Sandy, the self is usually the first thing to go in the effort to get love from others.

Self-denial is a form of protection from those basic hurts of early childhood. Unconsciously, these people remember how they felt when they asked for things and were repeatedly turned down. It was a frustration they had to endure, since showing their true feelings toward a parent on whom they depended was dangerous and apt to end in punishment or fears of being unloved, abandoned, or isolated.

Money martyrs are more likely to be women who have little money, who identify strongly with their mothers who were careful with money, and who weren't taught how to make or manage money when they were young.

One especially ironic version of money martyrdom involves earning just enough to stay afloat, and balancing accounts without having anything left over. Walking a financial tightrope provides a certain hard-to-define excitement for the money masochist. Any minor crisis could send her crashing to the ground, and that fact gets the adrenaline pumping. Staying on the tightrope becomes more important than enjoying life.

The self-denier can honestly explain her lack of self-indulgence by the tiny margin of safety she has created, but what she is really protecting herself from are the dangers that come with new and more enjoyable ways of living.

The first thing martyrs must do in order to learn to enjoy life and feel more secure, both emotionally and financially, is to admit their desire to loosen up. Once they are honest with themselves, they can actually take "baby steps" toward a less restrictive, less self-denying lifestyle.

Baby Steps

Here are some examples of modest but effective actions that have helped super-savers (like Suzanne) and money martyrs (like Sandy) learn to make their lives—and those of their nearest and dearest—more enjoyable. If their stories sound extremely familiar to you, and seem to reflect your own situation, you should probably consider incorporating these steps into your own life.

- Take stock of your income and assets so that you won't feel poor if you're really not.

- Make a point of being kind and nurturing to yourself in some tangible way every day.

- Remind yourself that there's nothing wrong with buying things at full, non-discounted retail prices every now and then.

- Find specific times during the day to repeat silent messages to yourself that reinforce the notion that you don't have to deprive yourself to feel good.

- Buy things you can afford even if items you're replacing aren't worn out completely.

- Stop yourself when you start thinking thoughts such as, "I really don't need this," "I'll make do and wait until after-Christmas sales," or "This isn't worth the money even though I like it." Focus on something else.

- Compliment yourself for whatever small, medium, or large risk you took that came out better than you expected.

- Keep a written list of things you like about yourself, and add to it each chance you get.

- Experiment with activities such as impulse buying, treating someone else to dinner, trying a new personal service, giving away some clothes that are still serviceable but out of date, or replacing some long-suffering household item with a trendy new model.

- After buying what you need in the supermarket, buy something inexpensive that you'd simply like to have such as a magazine, a dessert, or some candy. If you're on a diet, get a new gadget or try a new juice flavor instead. Try some fruits or vegetables you hardly ever or never buy. Get a new cookbook so you can prepare the veggies and fruits in new ways. Treat yourself to some new spice while you're at it.

- Refresh your classic wardrobe with a new accessory or two. Try an unusual color, and get a pair of shoes to match.

- Buy a book of your own for a change instead of going to the library.

- Buy your own newspaper instead of peeking at your neighbor's before he or she wakes up.

- Buy fresh flowers instead of potting avocado pits and pineapple tops. Don't buy flowers for the express purpose of drying them out and keeping them around for years in vases made from recycled wine bottles.

- Set aside a percentage of your savings for a mini-vacation over the next three-day weekend.

- Sign up for an adult-education class.

■ Eat out in an ethnic restaurant you've never risked experimenting with, or make some exotic specialty from scratch. Once you've developed the main course, consider throwing a party with an ethnic theme. Combine your homemade efforts with some treats you actually buy in a store.

The Bargain Hunter: Claire's Story

Claire lives on the modest salary of a magazine editor, but she has managed to accumulate dozens of cashmere sweaters, countless pairs of shoes, and enough antique jewelry to wear a different piece every day of the month. She didn't inherit a bundle. She just happens to have a remarkable knack for finding the very best buy.

Claire's shopper's eye is so expert, her friends joke, that she can spot a designer coat hidden in a thrift shop rack from five hundred paces. Like Suzanne and Sandy, Claire never spends money on personal service "luxuries" such as a taxi during rush hour. She's been known to get angry if family obligations require her to pay for a hotel room. However, unlike the previous two Security Seekers, Claire *does* enjoy the act of spending money, even a big chunk at once. But, there's a catch. In order for Claire to buy something, it generally has to represent an incomparable bargain. In Claire's case, it's not so much the game being hunted, but the thrill of the chase that matters. The size of the markdown, more than the item purchased, is what provides her with the addictive thrill.

If December 26th falls on a workday, Claire will take the day off so she can make the rounds of the after-Christmas sales, sweeping up bargains the moment her favorite boutiques open their doors. In the spring, she rents a car on weekends to drive through the towns on Long Island that have the best yard sales. During the summer, she makes an annual pilgrimage to the outlet stores in Freeport, Maine. Far from buying on impulse, Claire maps out a shopping trip as if it were a commando raid. To avoid overheating while on reconnaissance inside stores, she wears a jacket rather than a coat. She brings along the smallest shoulder bag she owns so she doesn't get tired. To speed up clothing changes, she wears a dress she can slip off and put back on in a matter of seconds. Claire always has a plan of attack, and she always knows what she's looking for.

Claire's friend, Roberta, used to accompany her on shopping trips occasionally, but she says she won't go any more. "It wasn't any fun," Roberta recalls, and she sounds a little surprised. "Whenever I got tired or thirsty, and wanted to take a break, Claire got mad. Once I found shoes that were an unbelievable deal, pricewise, but I wasn't sure they were comfortable. Claire said, 'Grab them. How can you go wrong?' Another time I asked her about a designer coat she had gotten quite excited about, but that I had never seen her wear after she bought it. She just said, 'Oh, that,' and shrugged a little. Sometimes I wonder what she's really shopping for."

As Roberta suspected, the time and energy some women pour into bargain hunting may indicate unresolved psychological problems. When the size of the discount matters more than anything else; when bargain items get hung in the closet and never emerge again; when super shoppers get rid of their white elephants by fobbing them off on friends as gifts; then bargain hunting is probably something other than an innocuous pastime.

Claire is a bargain hunter, but not in the way you usually associate with that term. Her insatiable desire to purchase is fueled not by a desire for things, but by a seemingly boundless urge to "beat the seller." Beneath the glee at making a rare "find" there may lie guilt at having figuratively gotten a real steal.

In Claire's case, bargain hunting offers a way to compensate for past emotional and material deprivations. When Claire was growing up, she felt her mother favored her brother, a talented track star. His trophies were proudly displayed on the mantelpiece, but Claire's straight A's barely won a word of praise. Her perfectionist mother demanded politeness, model table manners, and a spic-and-span room from Claire, and she spanked her daughter for even tiny infractions. Her father, whom she loved very much, read to her a great deal, and listened appreciatively to the stories Claire wrote. He died of emphysema when Claire was 14. Shortly thereafter, the family experienced serious financial problems. To keep up appearances, Claire's mother taught her how to buy at auctions and thrift shops.

These days, Claire loves her work, although she worries a lot about the instability in the magazine business. For seven years, she lived with a boyfriend, John, but when she finally worked up the courage to ask him about increasing their level of commitment, he left. Two years later, she knows she still hasn't recovered from this major disappointment.

Claire doesn't acknowledge any feelings of abandonment related to her father's death, nor does she appear to see how bargain-hunting helps her to feel that she is finally "evening the score." All she can accept is that her unending quest to get the very best deal seems to have become a permanent part of her routine. Claire can't really make up for what was missing in her life, but when she shops, she tries.

For some people, bargain hunting is a way to prove that they can survive in a cruel world. After all, they know how to get true value from their money, and they can make that money stretch farther than just about anyone else. The "hunt" isn't a way to run a household efficiently so much as a way to make up for deprivations in childhood. For the bargain hunter, money is often compensation for early deprivation in life.

Sometimes bargain hunters get shortchanged with poor-quality goods that were bought because they were drastically marked down. This can be a particularly aggravating experience for someone who feels that she has already spent enough of her time losing out emotionally. When the things that money can buy are as unreliable as people, a certain emptiness sets in.

There are people who bargain hunt in the way Claire does only after Christmas, or only during the summer sale season in July. Some only go to discount stores; others only to Madison Avenue boutiques. Flea markets, fire sales, auctions, yard sales, wholesale outlets, and thrift shops are other favorite places for the bargain hunters.

Everybody has experienced the pleasure of getting a bargain; think of when you get a great deal. When the sale price is considerably less than the original one, you probably think, "They don't know the real value of this item, but I do. The shopkeeper is not as clever as I am." This kind of experience is a temporary self-esteem booster, but it doesn't last. For the majority of shoppers, that's no problem. However, for people who become caught up in the process, like Claire, the cycle has to be repeated. The point is not to get a specific item or service, but rather to compensate for old letdowns.

The Compulsive Collector: Aline's Story

Visitors to Boston know of Isabella Stewart Gardner because of her passion for collecting. As the twentieth century dawned, she turned her grand home into a showplace for European fine art and furnishing. She was so proud of everything she amassed that she offered her house and its contents to the public, on the condition that nothing be changed or rearranged. Even when thieves stole twelve priceless paintings in 1990, caretakers were not allowed to hang anything else in their places.

Visitors to Rochester, New York, learn about Margaret Woodbury Strong because of her similar drive for collecting. As a rich only child early in the nineteenth century, she was allowed to fill up one bag per shopping excursion. Figuring that if she bought small items, she'd have more to show for her day, she concentrated on buying buttons, valentines, miniatures, and other small items. As a grown woman, Strong had the largest collection of dolls in the world, and she established her own museum to house her dolls and her many other possessions. Present-day researchers consider the Strong collection something of a treasure trove, but more than one visitor has found the apparent clutter of the place a bit intimidating.

When you have a strong drive to collect, the time you lavish on the contents of the collection is time showered on things, not people. It's interesting that the most acclaimed collectors tend to have been lonely as children, unable to connect emotionally with their peers and the adults around them.

Things don't talk back to you. They never make fun of you. They never argue. Even better, things give pleasure, take up time, and demand nothing more from you than arrangement, storage, and occasional dusting. Things give collectors a goal that may distract them from bothersome interpersonal experiences. After all, it's easier to talk about things than feelings. When you become a connoisseur, even of dolls or doorknobs, you can show off your knowledge of the topic and get a certain amount of admiration and respect from people. For people who don't relate easily to others, collecting offers opportunities to connect on a social level in some limited ways. Shy collectors can suddenly become quite charming in the presence of dealers, admirers, and other collectors.

Money comes into the picture since many collections represent investments that can increase in value. They can also provide a buffer of security against the prospect of economic collapse. Collecting is more respectable than penny-pinching. While you would never dream of filling a breakfront with a display of stock certificates, you can get the same message across, and display the most impeccable taste, by setting out your collection of china dinner bells or glass figurines. For some women, a collection highlights one's tastes, interests, and wealth simultaneously.

Aline collects Depression-era glass items. They're cheap, usable in a pinch, and they won't make her cry if any of them break. She keeps her favorite pieces in a credenza; others are piled up along a wall in her basement family room. Many of the vases and dishes carry memories for her, like the pieces that were marriage gifts for her parents. Her friend, Marta, collects the more expensive cut glass that pressed glass mimicked. Her collection is displayed on a well-lit wall unit shelf behind a glass door. The pieces fairly sparkle and say, "I'm the real thing, the good stuff." Aline spends a great deal of time with her collection, especially when things are stressful in her relationships with others. Some people think she spends a little too much time on her glass items.

When does an idiosyncrasy cross the line and become a compulsion? The answer isn't easy but it's worth noting that overreliance on the amassing of things, whether they are valuable or not, is classic Keeper behavior. If you can't stop cramming items into the house, if relationships with things take center stage in your lives, and start edging people into the background, it may be time to take a look inward and think about the psychic payoffs your things give you.

How Keepers Can Loosen the Grip of Insecurity

If you recognize yourself in any of the previous profiles, you may depend on money or valuable things to provide you with a sense of security that you need on a very basic level. Somewhere in your past, there may well have been a pattern which you were hurt or let down by someone you loved. It's possible that you concluded that you simply couldn't depend on important people in your life. Instead, you found that money provided a good substitute. With money you can take care of yourself and not have to rely on people who may not be dependable. Although you may have developed a deep conviction that the world is a cold, harsh place, now that you're an adult, you have the ability to question that belief. With a little experimenting, you may well find that not everyone will hurt you, and that people deserve more trust than you previously thought.

There's nothing wrong with money, bargains, or great deals *per se*—except when you depend on them for your self-esteem. The healthiest confidence and security comes from inside. Financial compensations in both the monetary and psychological senses of the word are a poor substitute. Fortunately, it's never too late to build a higher opinion of yourself. You can develop an inner sense of security by taking risks, meeting new challenges, and doing things that reinforce your confidence in your own ability to do things. Perhaps, in the process, you will get some bad advice, miss some great sales, or decrease your bank stash a bit. More likely, you'll discover new people and pastimes that give you pleasure and, little by little, you'll loosen up and enjoy life more.

Freeing yourself from compulsive saving, scrimping, bargain-hunting or collecting begins with recognizing that you *don't* have to remain at the mercy of your habits. By changing your life in small ways, you'll learn that catastrophes won't immediately occur. Gradually, you'll be able to lower the volume of that little voice in your head that fuels your compulsive activity. That voice demands that you rarely or never indulge yourself. That voice spews guilt. That voice hinders you from finding what you really want. Here are some ways to help quiet that voice.

- Find some part of your unhealthy pattern and try to break it. Keep a journal or tell a friend about your feelings and the actual results of your venture.

- Remember that how you think about life and money is within your control. Of course, lasting change doesn't occur overnight. Think of the process as removing a brick from a wall by loosening it here and there. Finally, after a great deal of jiggling, it comes out.

- Change because you want to, rather than because circumstances leave you no choice. Fear and desperation don't produce satisfying outcomes; a mature effort to overcome anxiety and outdated behavior bit by bit is likelier to result in long-term positive change. It takes at least five weeks to launch a new habit, so keep at it and reward yourself for each hurdle you overcome. Gradually the bricks will come down from your old wall.

The Security Shunner: Allison's Story

Strangely enough, those who score extremely low on the quiz that began this chapter may fall into what we might call an "anti-Keeper" category, one that leaves them subject to many related and unhealthy cycles that are quite closely related to those faced by Sandy, Claire, and Aline. I call these anti-Keepers—Security Shunners. They're the ones who don't seem to care about security. They simply avoid virtually all money thoughts, plans, and actions.

Mention the word "investments" to Allison and you'll see her eyes glaze over. "Money is boring," she'll scoff before changing the subject. At age 38, Allison has worked at a variety of jobs but her savings account never gets far above a two-month reserve. She's never bounced a check in her life and rarely lets her credit card balance pile up, but the idea of planning for the future sets her teeth on edge. Once, her friend Terri suggested that she think about setting aside some money in case of illness or unemployment. "You sound like my mother," Allison muttered. Terri's tale about a woman their age who'd had to apply for Social Security disability did terrify Allison for a few days, but she managed to put the worry out of her mind and go on as before.

Allison has always been healthy and is able to talk her way into just about any job she wants, but she hasn't given much thought to questions of long-term security. Most of Allison's relationships are with other women, and she has no particular desire for children or a house. When she was doing freelance window dressing, she went as long as a year and a half without health insurance, minimizing backup planning as a hang-up of her mother's. Yet, in the back of her mind, she assumes that if she ever got into serious trouble, her mother would bail her out. Allison's mother survived the Depression, though, and would never let her daughter forget it if she had to scrimp through her own long-awaited, comfortable retirement because her daughter failed to follow advice that had been repeated to her many times.

At some point in their thirties, most people wake up to the reality that they'll have to take care of themselves when they're old, and conclude that they ought to start planning for the future now. By rejecting that message, Allison is telling herself and the world, "I won't grow up."

Part of Allison's scorn for the whole idea of financial planning stems from having been sheltered from financial realities most of her life. She remembers her father, now divorced from her mother and estranged from the family, spending evenings calculating something or other about his stocks. She thought that was his hobby. In fact, her father's "hobby" paid for her college education. Allison's mother lives well in a paid-off house on interest from investments, Social Security, and a pension from the State partly because of Allison's father's planning and guidance. Unfortunately, neither of Allison's parents taught her the monetary facts of life. Did yours?

Allison is capable, inventive, and well paid, so she may sail through the next 25 years without any economic difficulties; by the same token, she may hit a bump in the road. In her ongoing rebellion, she's making a point to her parents (both classic Keepers), but she's also overlooking her own best interests. This pattern of studied obliviousness to financial matters is often one of the unfortunate corollaries of exposure to the Keeper mindset. When you rely on others in your lives to handle financial matters, you may start to assume that the security that they worked so hard to attain is a permanent part of the landscape. It isn't. Nobody can handle your money with the emotional "investment" better than you. If you grew up on the receiving end of the Keeper's mania for money and security, you should be careful to deal with any overcompensation in your own money patterns. You may also need to educate yourself, despite feelings that, in doing so, you are retracing the steps of a Keeper in your past. Others can be extremely helpful, but you have to be the ultimate decision maker. It is definitely not a good idea to hand over your money to others to manage.

Buying Security Sanely

If you recognize yourself as sharing Allison's "don't bore me with money" attitude, think about this:

- Although the gender gap is closing, women still earn, on average, only 72 cents for every dollar men earn.

- More women than men depend on Social Security alone for their income in retirement. However, since their earnings are lower, their Social Security benefits are less as well.

- If you wait until your mid-fifties to start saving seriously, you will have to save about 15 percent of your after-tax income to maintain your standard of living in retirement.

- Currently, nearly 75 percent of the elderly poor are women.

- Forty-two percent of baby boomer women say they'd rather have someone else take care of their retirement savings and investments, compared with 28 percent of men. These are the women most vulnerable to poor advice and broker exploitation.

When you consider the rate of divorce and the epidemic nonpayment of child support and alimony, you should realize how important it is for women to take control of their finances. As with security seekers, security shunners need to start small and add new behaviors to work toward the goals of emotional and financial security.

Here are some ideas to help you feel more secure with money. Odds are that your inclinations are fundamentally those of the Keeper. Once you begin the process, you will probably enjoy knowing that your money is growing.

- Start reading the business section of the newspaper at least once a week. Look up unfamiliar financial terms in the dictionary. Start reading personal finance magazines like *Money, Smart Money, Kiplinger's,* and *Worth* and get a subscription to one of them. Read the financial columns in women's magazines and pay more attention to the financial news on radio and television.

- Put your anxiety to work for you. Whenever you feel a passing worry about your future, take some action. Keep the name and number of a well-recommended financial planner by the phone and make an appointment when the urge strikes. When talking to your financial planner, ask him or her to discuss developing a portfolio that assumes that you're 10 or more years older than you actually are.

- Every month, stash away $50 or $100 in a separate account that you can't easily plunder.

- Ask friends your age in your income bracket what they have in the way of savings and investments. See what you can do to catch up with them.

- Keep in mind that building up a treasure trove doesn't mean you have to sacrifice your freedom. Even as you begin a program of saving, make sure you maintain some of your usual indulgences.

Some women find that as they take steps toward mastering money, they begin dancing on both sides of the street. They'll talk about their intentions, but they'll make a tepid approach rather than a true commitment to change. This ambivalence can sabotage your progress.

Keep in mind that deciding to take charge of your money can only lead to a better situation. On those days when the fear of taking charge looms higher up in your reality, you can weigh down the opposite end of the seesaw by saying "Stop" to irrational fears that may come up such as, "I'm too stupid to do this." Try saying out loud, "I want to take charge of my money." Worry doesn't work, and denial doesn't take care of you. So don't give either of these options any more of your energy.

Chapter 4

The Love Buyers

Jennifer's Story

ennifer lives in the suburbs. She's very concerned with how things look: the windows must be washed, the landscaping has to be professionally done, and the gleaming luxury car must be parked in the driveway where everyone can see it. Jennifer's husband wants to let the neighbors know that he earns a good salary, so she makes sure that she and her husband have the best of everything, in the most ostentatious and public way possible. When the couple entertains, Jennifer makes sure the guests enjoy first-class food and decorations.

But there's a problem. For all the interest Jennifer shows in spending money, she has very little idea of how much is available. Jennifer is maxing out the couple's lines of credit in order to support a lifestyle that's the most opulent on the block—a lifestyle that she and her husband cannot afford. Her husband has been able to juggle credit cards for the most part, but he is finding it increasingly difficult to make more than the minimum payments. On several occasions, Jennifer has not told her husband about some of the bills she's incurred. More than once, she's even burned the bills the moment they arrived in the mail. Sometimes Jennifer tackles the stack of bills and sometimes her husband does, but most of the time, neither one is really in control. Trying to keep up with the Joneses can make you do strange things.

Jennifer is maintaining an image, not only for her neighbors, but for her family and its expectations. As she grew up, it was made clear to her that she had to be the "one to succeed." She was supposed to be the best dressed, furnish her home tastefully, and drive an expensive foreign car. No one instilled in Jennifer the notion of gradually working her way to levels of achievement. Jennifer spent her life fulfilling and maintaining the unspoken, external-success fantasy that was so important to her parents—on borrowed money. At some point, Jennifer equated not having status symbols with letting her family down. She also wanted to repeat the cycle of attention, recognition, compliments, and approval she always got when she made major purchases. She transferred the same sense of obligation to her husband, who was astounded to learn that her purchasing patterns were based, in part, on a desire not to disappoint him.

After a long period of self-examination, Jennifer was able to turn around her behavior. She is more realistic now about what she really wants and how to go about getting what she needs. A certain "reprogramming" was necessary, and her husband helped out on this score: When Jennifer stays within the family budget, she gets lots of positive reinforcement from her husband. When she consults her own gut instinct, and stops to consider whether she's buying something for her own benefit or for the benefit of other people, she's taking a giant step toward a positive change in attitude. This change will pay off emotionally as well as financially.

Jennifer is a Love Buyer. She uses money as a replacement for what is lacking in other aspects of her emotional life.

For the Love Buyer, money provides a boost to one's self-esteem and personal reinforcement that is or was once lacking in interactions with others. Purchasing something serves, for members of this group, as a replacement for the natural affection and self-confidence that arises from strong primary relationships with other people.

Here are some more questions that explore your attitudes toward money, purchases, and relationships. Even if you are not a Love Buyer, you will want to take this test to get a better understanding of the people in your life who may approach relationships from a Love Buyer point of view.

The Love Buyer's Quiz

1. How often do you go clothes shopping?

    a) More than five times a month

    b) About once a month

    c) At the end of each season, but usually when I get around to it, since it's not a top priority.

2. Which of the following statements best describes your outlook?

    a) I feel a real lift when I go shopping. It's one of the times when I feel best about myself.

    b) Shopping is a great way to get your mind off something if you're feeling mad or frustrated.

    c) Shopping can be fun, but sometimes enough is enough.

3. You're under oath: Have you ever shoplifted?

    a) Yes.

    b) I've thought about it seriously, but no.

    c) Never even came close.

4. You're getting ready to give a friend a fairly expensive gift. Which of the following statements comes closest to describing the way you would feel about this?

    a) He/she had better make a big deal about it at the party. It's the best brand around.

    b) Maybe now he/she will show me some appreciation for a change.

    c) I hope the color's right.

5. Which of the following reasons seems to you to be the most likely justification you would offer for an unplanned expense?

    a) It's perfect—it's exactly what I want, and I deserve it.

    b) It's not going to be here forever, and the price is right.

    c) This is an emergency situation.

6. Your boyfriend, who has been planning to take you to an expensive restaurant upon his return from a business trip, realizes that he has no cash and no bank card. He left them in his other suit, which has been misrouted to another city due to a luggage mix-up at the airport. You cannot afford to pay for this restaurant even on a short-term basis. Which of the following options would probably be your immediate reaction? (Be honest)

    a) Mention how unhappy you are, how much you were looking forward to the dinner, and how thoughtless it was of your boyfriend to misplace his wallet.

    b) Suggest an alternate restaurant, one where you can afford to pick up the tab, but tell your boyfriend he owes you one.

    c) Grab a couple of hot dogs from a sidewalk vendor and take a walk together.

7. Which of the following comes closest to describing your financial philosophy?

    a) I want what I want, when I want it. If money isn't for enjoying now, why do I put up with so much grief for it now?

    b) You've got to splurge every once in a while.

    c) Save for a rainy day.

8. When was the last time you bought the same article of clothing in multiple colors or styles?

    a) Within the last two months

    b) Two to three months ago

    c) More than three months ago (Or: I can't recall ever having done this.)

9. How many times have you bought a kitchen tool, small appliance, or article of clothing that still had the price tag or original packaging attached after more than two months?

   a) More than once

   b) Rarely

   c) Never, to my knowledge

Scoring

Give yourself 5 points for every "a" answer, 3 points for every "b" answer, and 1 point for every "c" answer. Here's how to interpret your score:

36–50 points:	For you, money and love are intertwined.
26–35 points:	You may find it hard to separate money and love in some situations.
10–25 points:	You have a relatively mature approach when it comes to separating love issues from monetary issues.

Money Lovers, Money Spenders

Love, not the love of money, is the motivating principle for the Love Buyer. If you scored high on this quiz, you're probably looking to money to provide what's missing in your life—or at least what you believe is missing. When you don't feel good about yourself, you may confuse money for love and approval. You may use the cost of a gift as a barometer of how much you care about somebody or how much they care about you. There is certainly more money than love in this world, and it is easy to understand how you would try to guarantee acceptance, flattery, and positive responses by being quick with an open pocketbook.

The truth is, though, that money doesn't really buy friendships, happiness, or self-esteem. What the Love Buyer actually gets is a quick fix, a brief, short-lived boost to his or her self-esteem which must be repeated frequently to maintain the level of comfort he or she grows used to. If this pattern sounds like part of your life, you owe it to yourself to find other ways to enjoy feelings of self-worth. There are many better and longer-lasting ways to feel good about yourself rather than relying on money. These alternatives also have the advantage of being far less likely to drive you into the poorhouse.

This is a consumer society, one that encourages you to equate purchasing with pleasure. To a certain extent, everyone is susceptible to the patterns exhibited by the Love Buyer. For most people, however, purchases are not intertwined with deep-rooted issues of self-esteem on an everyday basis. If this cycle has you overloading credit cards, hiding bills, and engaging in other ultimately self-defeating behavior in order to keep up with the Joneses, you need to stop and ask yourself whether it's worth it to live under a constant black cloud of debt in an attempt to buy what money really can't deliver.

Don't Bet on the Prince to Rescue You

Attitude is the key for success or failure. Gail's is, "I need it now." What does she need? She has silk blouses in a rainbow of colors—but not a dollar in her IRA. For Gail, having something tangible, something she can put her hands on, is what counts. She resents it when anyone suggests that she should save for her future, because her true objective is to find a husband to look out for her interests. Her idea of taking the best possible care of herself is to dress well enough to attract a man.

Gail has done what women over the centuries did. She abdicates responsibility for her future and believes some unknown man is responsible for that. In the not-so-distant past, women's security, status, and life depended on a man's earning capability. With education, career, and job opportunities, and the very real possibility of being self-supporting, women are finally free of this need, which amounted to bondage in many cases. Too often, women link their self-image to the degree to which they attract men.

Gail would be better off if she found ways to send positive messages to herself about her own good qualities, messages that have nothing to do with money. Hoping that other people will give her reinforcement, based on her appearance, is a poor replacement for developing a strong self-image on her own. Her self-confidence would be a most attractive "vibe" to draw others to her.

Filling a Hole

For many Love Buyers, childhood was marked by more money than affection. Affluence works against some families. It often leaves emotional voids, encourages intense competitiveness, and encourages children to define success primarily in monetary terms. Some parents who are upwardly mobile feel that children get in the way of all the work that has to be done, so they buy things to compensate for their absence or emotional distance. Others decide that they want their kids to have the best of everything. Both of these approaches lead children to develop some strange attitudes toward money.

In the case of families with upwardly mobile parents who are distant emotionally, it is not uncommon for children to feel unwanted, or even unlovable and worthless. They grow up seeing money as a reward and the lack of it as a punishment. Because these children never felt unconditionally loved, they have a difficult time loving themselves, and they often cannot show love to others. When they want love, they assume that they have to buy it. They see love as a commodity like any other, one that always has a price tag.

In the case of children whose parents vow to supply "all the best," there is often an expectation of ever greater levels of reward. For some children, all that's necessary to obtain something is to ask. It's not surprising, then, that asking is just about all they learn to do. When parents make a habit of indulging their children, or try to "keep peace in the household" by never saying no, they unwittingly teach them to continue this sense of entitlement. This leads to a feeling of emotional betrayal if the rewards should ever stop coming in adulthood, and that in turn leads to some major difficulties in one's adult relationships.

Maria

Maria works all week—and shops all weekend.

She grew up in an affluent household, one in which material rewards were a primary means of communication. When she got good grades, she got things as a reward. When she didn't do what she was supposed to do, she felt she was frozen out of the family. In both situations, however, emotional demonstrativeness was rare. Maria's family gave her little encouragement to pursue her talents, and she got minimal enjoyment out of pursuing interests for her own pleasure. When she frequently was complimented for her nice accessories and clothing, she felt great. Now she has to shop to get that feeling.

This "have to" feeling is crucial in differentiating compulsive shopping from the variety of shopping with which most people are familiar. Just as an alcoholic needs a drink, an overeater has to have ice cream, and a drug addict must get a fix, the shopaholic's spending habits are chronic. Although they may be satisfied temporarily, they must be repeated.

Instead of thinking through a troublesome situation or talking about the feelings that situation stirs up, the compulsive shopper will swing into action. To feel more in control, this type of shopper feels there is no alternative to hitting the stores.

Help for Maria lies in learning to enjoy the work week more by being more involved in what she does, and taking pleasure from the process of her ongoing projects, rather than the end results. Maria tends to look toward her boss to make or break her day, just as she looked to her parents for rewards or punishments. As she gradually stops allowing him to have this power, she'll notice that she can keep from having her disposition ruined—and her need to shop will diminish.

If Maria can be more positive about her own efforts, she'll have more energy and enjoy greater productivity. A more positive outlook will help her understand that, while it's common to experience her colleagues as members of her family, the reality is that they are not her family, and they don't have the power to hurt her in the same way that members of her own family did. In time, Maria can assimilate this lesson and break free of the self-destructive shopping cycles that now imprison her.

> No one has to continue old patterns that don't work. Control comes with figuring out new, more effective ways to cope with the old feelings that have stayed with you over the years.

Kim

Kim has a "closet issue." She is one of those women who goes shopping regularly but never throws anything out. Her closets are so jammed that she can't get anything in or out of them. Some of the clothes still have the price tags on them.

The pleasures of shopping for items, trying them on, having a sales person who recognizes and flatters her, and buying them, all give Kim a feeling of validation and self-worth. It's not surprising, then, that Kim makes a habit of being trendy when it comes to apparel. She has to have the latest color and styles, and if short skirts are fashionable, she has to have all the right shoes and accessories necessary for the new look. Kim has become so accustomed to the notion of being perfectly well-dressed and up-to-date that she has to have everything new all at once. The idea of wearing last year's coat with this year's outfits is almost heretical to Kim.

For all of Kim's carefully coordinated exterior, she is deeply divided on the inside. Her overriding need to present the "correct" front is motivated by a crippling fear that she is basically inadequate as a person. Even her high-powered career as a headhunter doesn't serve as much of a positive influence. Kim makes a very good salary, but she feels overwhelmingly guilty about how much of it she spends. To offset the guilt, she'll take a bus home instead of a cab after a spending splurge. Then she feels better, and she is ready to spend again the next time she goes shopping. Sometimes her friends joke that she has so many clothes that she ought to hang a sign outside her apartment that reads "Boutique."

Slowly, Kim has started to reverse some of her negative patterns by realizing that even if she doesn't have the latest outfit, she will still be accepted for herself. That is, after all, what counts in the final analysis. By working to find and notice things within herself that she can be proud of, instead of superficial things, Kim is taking steps in the direction of positive change.

Kim has had a number of fights with her husband over the years on the topic of "selfishness." Once he remarked rather testily that "only one of us gets to wear your new fur coat, but both of us can take a vacation." Actually, "true" selfishness, the kind of attention that focuses on taking care of the most precious part of you—your Self—is good. It's self-centeredness—believing that your interests and only your interests are the ones that matter—that you should avoid.

Overcoming the "Buying-for-Self-Esteem" Cycle

- Get help through Debtor's Anonymous or a therapist.

- Sort out what feelings are surfacing to create the urge to splurge. If necessary, talk to a professional about your feelings.

- Ask yourself, "What is missing, emotionally speaking, in my life?" Could it be feelings of self-worth, validation, appreciation, or confidence?

- Once you identify those gaps, ask yourself how you could get those without going shopping. Develop a list of challenges, and as you meet them, congratulate and appreciate yourself. Pat yourself on the back every day for small, medium, and large things you did that make you proud of yourself.

- Is there someone who knows how to "push all your buttons"? Make a list of ways you can handle the frustration or rage you may feel toward that person that don't involve spending money.

- Learn to view saving money as the practice of satisfying later needs, not as a deprivation.

- Allow yourself to feel the gratification of financial responsibility.

- Envision yourself talking things over with your boss, husband, teenager, or any other important person in your life. See yourself outlining the situation as it appears to you. See yourself discussing what you want, what they want, and offering a solution for discussion.

- Become sensitive to self-enhancing feelings, attitudes, and deeds. Tell yourself out loud every day in the bathroom mirror what these things are. Build self-esteem by giving yourself approval.

- Perform "plastic surgery" on your credit cards—cut them up!

- Use cash when shopping.

- Take a walk instead of going to stores on your lunch hour.

■ Alter your commuting route if tempting stores are located on the way to work or home.

Lisa

Lisa has accumulated $8,000 worth of debt on her credit card. Since she pays the minimum each month, she'll be paying off that debt for fourteen years, and will have paid double for all of her purchases by the time she's finished. She's unable to knock down the debt significantly. Lisa is frightened and sick to her stomach. She's already gotten her mother involved and has borrowed some money over the last year from her, but Mom has warned her that she shouldn't expect any more help. Lisa had to swallow her pride to ask for money in the first place, and now she notices a distinct difference in how often she and her mother talk.

Lisa has to keep her resentful feelings about her relationship with her mother to herself. She thinks, "My friends' parents help them out when they need it. Aren't parents supposed to be there for times like this? My mom can afford to help me, but I guess she thinks she's building my character by limiting me. In the meantime, I'm trying valiantly to make some extra money by checking coats at a local restaurant and waiting tables on the weekends to scratch some money together. I'm overwhelmed and have no life beyond work. The only character I'm building is a tired and depressed one."

As a child, Lisa wasn't taught to save, to live within her means, or to forego material pleasures. It's not too late to learn, but the way she's learning the lesson now is affecting her relationship with her mother in a negative way. The principles she's finally mastering feel more like punishments than valuable, lifelong skills her mother wants her to learn. She's been cut off "cold turkey" and has to learn the hard way that excessive personal debt is bad news.

While the Baby Boomers represent the most affluent generation in history, they have the lowest rate of savings in the industrial world. For many of today's "I want it all now" spenders, it has been easier to charge what they desire at the moment than to save for it, and the result has been some very impressive mountains of personal debt.

Admitting that you're over your head in debt can be a shameful experience. You may even prefer to admit you're an alcoholic or have been unfaithful to your spouse than suffer the humiliation of letting others know that you can't keep your financial house in order. With alcohol, you can blame your environment, your parents, or the disease, but with overspending, it's hard to get away from the fact that you were the one who bought all those things.

HOW DO YOU KNOW IF YOU'RE IN TROUBLE?

- If you use one credit card to pay off another

- If you don't open your bills since you figure you can't pay them anyway

- If you rely on fantasies of being rescued by a windfall inheritance or a rich man who wants to marry you

- If you find yourself dipping into your savings or considering consolidating your debts by taking out a loan

If one or more of these signs apply to you, then you should probably start a serious debt-reduction program. Don't think that by ignoring the problem, it will go away. Denial is the first sign of trouble. One woman, I am told, used the last one hundred dollars worth of credit on her MasterCard to buy an answering machine, so she wouldn't have to talk to the bill collectors who bothered her! This is denial in its purest form.

Facing up to the problem means you'll have to take a look at the figures. Seeing in black and white the extent of the damage can be traumatic. However, without keeping a daily diary of expenses and categorizing them at the end of the month, it's hard to know where the money is going.

Laura

Laura was astonished to see that she was shelling out about $400 a month for lunches, after-work drinks, and dinners. She wanted to be part of the gang that socialized after the hectic work day at the local eatery. "It was fun to unwind with everyone, and I needed to feel that I was accepted as part of the group, but I see now that hanging out is expensive," she explained.

Laura didn't give up the after-work fun, but she did forego alcohol. "I realized that I didn't have to stop enjoying myself or give my life to my creditors. By not drinking, I was able to save half of what it was I was used to spending, and I didn't really miss the drinks. Also, instead of expensive entrees, I'd order an appetizer and a small salad, and I was fine. I didn't feel stuffed, hung over, or poor either."

Changes in spending don't necessarily have to be draconian, but you do have to decide on your priorities. There is always something you can cut back on—your job is to find out what it is. Taking buses instead of taxis, buying bouquets of dried flowers instead of fresh ones, repairing shoes instead of buying new ones, and brown-bagging lunches are a few ways to cut expenses painlessly.

There are rewards for paying off debt. You will not see an appreciable change for a while, but you will get some satisfaction from knowing that you are working on whittling down the debt. When you wake up at 4 a.m., you can reassure yourself that you are going through a temporary rough period. The tough times will end because you are conscientiously working on paying off your debts. As long as you are doing something about the problem, you can rest a little easier. Wanting things to be under control and feeling more secure are the goals to keep in focus. When tinges of deprivation seep into your consciousness, banish those thoughts with a one-liner about your goals.

OVERCOMING CHRONIC DEBT PROBLEMS

- Take the initiative. Notify your creditors that you intend to pay them and work out an arrangement to pay what you can afford each month. Most serious credit problems arise when people make the mistake of attempting to ignore creditors. By explaining that you are working to pay back what you owe, you will regain control of the situation.

- If you owe the Internal Revenue Service money, by all means, do not delay in contacting them to discuss your situation. Set up a plan and stick to it. By doing so, you'll avoid further penalties and angst. Don't ignore notices from the IRS under any circumstances!

- Consider seeing a psychotherapist who can help you to put the words to your buying and debting behavior.

- Go to Debtors Anonymous or AA meetings in your area.

- Envision how life will be with your finances under control.

- Avoid being harsh with yourself for getting into trouble.

- Remind yourself that this difficult period is a temporary one.

- Explore how your need for love enters into your spending habits— since emotional triggers are often the biggest problem.

- Perform "plastic surgery" on your credit cards—cut them up!

- Postpone major new purchases. If you're tempted to buy something on the installment plan, calculate exactly how long it will take you to pay off the new purchase.

- Use cash whenever possible.

- Comparison shop for everything. This will help you overcome any tendency to shop impulsively.

- Stay positive. It's your life, no matter what your financial situation looks like.

. . . And Then There's Gambling

If ever there was a financial pattern with the capacity to destroy relationships, it's gambling. The downward spiral of compulsive gambling is usually associated with men, but the self-destructive aspects of this problem for women is rising. The image of the "macho man" betting at blackjack, figuring the odds for football pools, and spending hours at the racetrack is a familiar one, but women who compulsively feed quarters into slot machines for hours on end, or try their luck at the local bingo hall, represent different aspects of the same social problem.

The number of women who gamble is growing, thanks to the increasing number of state-sponsored lotteries and other gaming opportunities. Women tend to be quiet gamblers who keep a low profile, but they are just as capable of ruining their lives through compulsive attachments to games of chance as are men. Generally, they are trusted employees who might have access to company money, or family people who divert small sums of money from the household cookie jar week after week. Women who work and have family responsibilities don't have much time to gamble, but there are many who bet every day with small sums of money and who keep this "habit" hidden for years.

While men look for "Lady Luck" to smile on them with a big win, women tend to be low rollers who are seeking daily escape from an unhappy life situation. They use gambling as a temporary way out of difficult situations such as divorce, absentee husbands, empty-nest syndrome, or the loss of a close friend or relative. Loneliness is the key word here.

For many women, gambling is the only part of their lives that allows them to feel as though they are in control. They may see themselves as the victims of other peoples' expectations, or as having been abandoned by others. In these situations, gambling serves as a stress reducer that helps them get through the daily grind. Sometimes, the habit carries serious costs.

Gambling can slowly take over a woman's life. The underlying fears and feelings of inadequacy continue to bubble to the surface, and the result is easy to predict: more and more gambling to numb the pain. Women who have low self-esteem, feel depressed, inadequate, misunderstood, and unappreciated find that they have only complicated these discomforts by adding another burden: how to find the time and money to gamble.

The woman who is a compulsive gambler is involved in a dangerous cycle, one that can expand for as long as she allows it. Sooner or later, when her children experience trouble at school, or socially, when her relationships fall apart, when money is found missing at work, or when she's confronted with the empty cookie jar at home, she'll either hit bottom and admit that she needs help, or go back to gambling even more.

Approximately 5 percent of the American population are compulsive gamblers. That comes to about 12 million people whose lives are characterized by chaos, instability, and insecurity. They bounce back and forth from anger and rage, to depression. They are prisoners of feelings of helplessness and hopelessness. Their lives are out of control because they are constantly preoccupied with finding the time and money to recoup their losses. Not infrequently, they lose everything, including their own freedom.

Unfortunately, there is limited help available for gamblers whether they are men, women, or adolescents of either gender. There are treatment programs, Gamblers Anonymous groups, and therapists who have experience with this problem, but, on the whole, society is still behind in recognizing and addressing this problem.

Since the issues related to this problem are similar to those of other compulsions, twelve-step programs (such as Alcoholics Anonymous), can be helpful to those who need help but can't find a program in their area targeted specifically to the needs of compulsive gamblers.

DO YOU HAVE A GAMBLING PROBLEM? THE ANSWER IS "YES" IF YOU:

- Find yourself thinking constantly about how you can get the money you need to gamble or repay gambling debts

- Gamble more money or for a longer period of time than you originally intended

- Need to increase the size of your bets in order to feel excited

- Feel irritable if you can't gamble

- Lose money repeatedly and then try to win back what you lost

- Try to stop gambling and find that you can't

- Find that you're more socially confident when gambling

- Gamble instead of seeing friends, pursuing interests, or working

- Continue to gamble even though you're in debt

Chapter 5

Power Seekers

Two Couples' Stories

*S*heila is a corporate lawyer who lives with Bob, a television pro-
ducer. She makes many times his salary, and ends up paying the
larger chunk of the bills when they go out to eat or spend a weekend
together.

"I'm not looking for a man to provide for me," Sheila says. "Fortunately, I can afford to pick a man regardless of how much he earns. I
don't mind plunking down extra money because I want to stay at nice
places and eat well. We talk about money sometimes. It's usually
with humor, to take the edge off of the anxiety, I guess. Part of me
wants to be taken care of, and when I feel that way, I'll ask Bob to
plan an evening or weekend. We'll do something simple, and that's
fine with me."

Not all relationships are as easygoing as Sheila's and Bob's, however. Alicia and Ron found they had big problems after she got a raise
and a bonus that, taken together, brought her salary to his level.
Alicia was jubilant at first and looked forward to spending money on
the dining room set they'd held off buying. She thought she'd surprise
Ron for his birthday by getting it.

Ron was surprised, all right, and angry, too, that Alicia had gone
ahead without his input to purchase this big-ticket item. Later, he
said, "I was mad that she didn't consult me. It also seemed that she

stopped asking me for help after she got her raise . . ." Apparently, Ron saw this emerging pattern as a threat.

Alicia acknowledged that her sexual relationship with Ron "seriously disintegrated" after her career blossomed. "I really felt terrific about myself since I knew I could take care of myself," she said. "The more I worked, though, the less attention he gave me. It felt like he was retaliating and letting me know that I couldn't have everything my way. He was going to dole out attention and control our sex life."

Although one could make an argument that Alicia's way of breaking the news to Ron about her raise wasn't the most thoughtful, I think this couple's story illustrates what can happen when the male in the relationship feels the need to exercise a level of authority and control that is out of scale with reality. Control freaks may have their careers in order, but they often make choices that have adverse effects on their loved ones as Bob's sudden choice to attempt to control the couple's sex life illustrates.

Controllers like Bob may also stifle their children, walk out on mates or force them to leave, and alienate friends—all because they feel threatened, often out of all proportion to the situation. Even though they usually manage to get things done their way, with all the details in order, they suffer from lack of trust, a fear of any exposure of their flaws, and a pervasive sense of vulnerability.

For Ron, a Power Seeker, money provides the means to control people. Members of this group tend to feel that financial control is the same thing as control of human emotions and events, and they often manipulate their loved ones by giving or withholding material rewards. Many, and perhaps most, Power Seekers had troublesome childhoods marked by feelings of humiliation. They never want to feel that way again, but it's all right for others to be treated as they were.

Below are some more questions that explore attitudes toward money, purchasing, and relationships. Even if you are not a Power Seeker, you will want to take this test—and review the answers that follow—to get a better understanding of the people in your life who may approach relationships from a Power Seeker point of view.

The Power Seeker's Quiz

1. Which of the following statements comes closest to describing the way you handle money?

  a) "Spend some, save some"

  b) "Easy come, easy go"

  c) "Hold on tight to those purse strings"

2. Which of the following statements comes closest to describing your purchasing philosophy?

  a) "Pay cash on the barrelhead"

  b) "Make occasional dips into credit reserves for important purchases"

  c) "Buy now, and pay as late as possible"

3. When you go shopping, what's most important to you?

  a) Getting a bargain

  b) Getting good sales help

  c) Getting exactly what you want

4. With which of the following statements would you most likely agree?

  a) "I buy only at sales. Why pay more?"

  b) "You can't get too wrapped up in planning. If I like it, I buy it."

  c) "Quality counts. I buy name-brand merchandise."

5. Which of the following items would you most likely buy yourself for a birthday present?

  a) A needed household article

  b) Bubble bath, cosmetics or cologne

  c) Something made out of silk, leather, gold, or silver

6. Which of these adjectives would your friends most likely apply to you?

   a) Consistent

   b) Easygoing

   c) Assertive

7. If you had to choose from one of the three options below, which would be closest to your idea of a dream home?

   a) Modest—but paid for

   b) Decorator's delight

   c) Penthouse

8. If you were being offered three different job opportunities, and each offered *one* of the following advantages, which offer would be most appealing to you?

   a) Security—good long-term potential

   b) Recognition—the opportunity to earn praise from your peers and the public

   c) Respect—a high position in the pecking order, and lots of status symbols

9. What was your childhood like?

   a) Happy

   b) Fairly happy

   c) Troubled

10. What kind of vacation do you prefer?

   a) Package tour

   b) Romantic cruise

   c) Offbeat adventure

Scoring

Give yourself 1 point for every "a" answer, 2 points for every "b" answer, and 3 points for every "c" answer.

10–17 points: You're pretty conservative, and you play things too close to the vest to qualify as a Power Seeker.

18–24 points: Although you may like the idea of being in control and taking charge from time to time, you tend to take a middle-of-the-road approach in most situations.

25–30 points: Competition doesn't scare you. You're a leader who likes things your way.

The Essentials of Unhealthy Power

Many Power Seekers are driven by rage arising from a pattern of painful experiences that occurred during their childhood. Their hurt has to do with early feelings of humiliation and weakness. They then learned that to cry, or even to show any feelings whatsoever, was a sign of weakness. Thanks to alcoholic, domineering, or otherwise authoritarian parents, many Power Seekers went through early life determined not to express their rage at the difficult situations they had to face as a way to show "strength." The humiliations these people endured, whether they arose from rejection, abuse, social isolation, or other sources, served as a motivation to "hedge all bets" so that they would never, under any circumstances, have to face humiliation again.

Some Power Seekers who fit the profile just outlined may try to cheat, manipulate, scheme, and skirt the outer reaches of both the law and social propriety. They may behave in outrageous ways in order to find out just where the edge of the law and tolerable behavior lies. It's likely, however, that many of these Power Seekers who are manipulators will get caught.

Every day, it seems, you hear news stories about lawyers, politicians, financial wizards, business tycoons, and even judges who behave as if they don't have to obey the rules that are designed to regulate the behavior of everyone else in society. The fact that large sums of money are often involved in these scandals may seem like these people can't get enough of it, but what they can't get enough of is power. They will do anything to avoid being in a vulnerable position ever again. Plus, they will do to others what was done to them. The irony, of course, is that when they are caught, they often suffer public humiliation on a grand scale. Ironically, manipulators are generally turned in by other manipulators.

By the same token, many wheeler-and-dealer Power Seekers may go on "pushing the envelope" for years. They are frequently charming enough to get their way, either because of their ability to talk a good game or their talent at presenting an attractive exterior. These people can often lie without showing the least sign of anxiety. A good many Power Seekers act as though there were two sets of rules—one for them and one for the rest of the world. Some get away with this assumption for the better part of a lifetime. Some don't.

For many Power Seekers, observing socially imposed limits is close to impossible, because they weren't taught as children what "no" meant. Quite a few Power Seekers learned early on in life how to go around parents, teachers, and others to get what they wanted, when they wanted. Not surprisingly, a certain arrogance often sets in among people whose important relationships are built on such a foundation. It is not uncommon to hear Power Seekers dismiss questions of morality with statements like, "There haven't been any problems yet." What they really mean, of course, is "I haven't been caught yet." To many of the people in this group, guilt feelings never seem to arise out of any action, and questions of right and wrong seem to be very easily rationalized.

R-E-S-P-E-C-T

Respect is extremely important to Power Seekers. As children, they were often expected to give respect to their elders, even in situations when the adults in the family deserved very little. In some cases, people who grow up to be Power Seekers were treated in an extremely dismissive manner as children. Their feelings, thoughts, ideas, or deeds were not considered valid or worthy of attention by the authority figures in their lives. As we know, entire ethnic groups have been treated as second-class citizens. This lack of acceptance motivates many to overcompensate. Often, that translates to piling up enough money to buy respect.

To be sure, money can buy respect in certain circles. But it can also lead to some unfortunate misconceptions about human relationships. If you don't do what some Power Seekers want you to do—if you don't offer them respect on the terms they define—you will be replaced. That goes for friends, subordinates, business associates, and, very often, wives and children, as well.

Power Seekers have to be in charge, dominant, and self-reliant. They were hurt by people in the past, and they have determined that they want "the upper hand" in all future relationships. This is the hand that does the spanking, and it's better to be in that position than to be the one who is "put down." To be put down is to be made into a child again, and perhaps a punished or humiliated one at that. Power Seekers know what that feels like and never ever want to feel that again.

Power Seekers often intimidate others with their fiery outbursts. They often put spouses on notice that if they, the Power Seekers, don't get their way, there's a good chance that a nasty volcano will erupt sometime soon. These people must be in control at all times, and if that means threatening or actually throwing fits, so be it.

It will come as no surprise to learn that many Power Seekers are very lonely, unhappy people. They may have the things worth having, the things associated with the "good life," but somehow they don't feel that they're the people worth being. Power Seekers often have difficulty relating well to others, because they have not developed the ability to compromise, or work things out.

Submissive types are often attracted to Power Seekers. Undemanding people are frequently the only ones who can tolerate being around these intimidating characters on a day-to-day basis. Over time, however, even a submissive friend or mate may question the real costs associated with being involved in such a relationship, and he or she may feel the instinct to take a stand at some point. Once the formerly submissive person speaks up, however, he or she risks being rejected or replaced.

Male Power, Female Power

Power still seems to be essential to men. Where the Power Seeker goes wrong is not in undertaking the *quest* for personal independence and control, but in the belief that control—typically, the limited kind of control measured by money—should extend to every facet of one's relationships with others. Rewards and punishments with money are par for the course.

On the one hand, women who take on such traits as part of their professional persona may be solidifying their claim to top management positions, and overcoming the unfortunate but widespread perceptions that women nag and cajole people into getting things done, and that they are not the "real decision makers" within the organization. However, women whose profiles indicate a tendency toward Power Seeker behavior have to play the political games.

Taking control of your own destiny is good. Doing so under the impression that you are entitled, as a result, to develop a series of relationships in which you communicate only on your own terms—or not at all—is unhealthy.

If you are involved in a long-term relationship with a Power Seeker, there is a very good chance that you will come to a point in your relationship where you must decide whether or not to take a stand. At this point, you will have to determine whether or not to take direct action to assure your own status as an equal partner in the relationship rather than as someone to be flirted with, bypassed, or talked down to when serious questions come up. Assuming personal control of your own life may well cost you both the relationship and the material rewards associated with it. This choice is likely to be an exceptionally difficult one for you to make, and it is one that will probably have unfortunate consequences attached to all possible outcomes. In making this difficult choice, you should remind yourself that the Power Seeker in your life is not the only one entitled to a sense of control and personal autonomy.

If you are a Power Seeker, you should understand that there are a number of hurdles awaiting you in your relationships with other people. These hurdles can be overcome only by a willingness on your part to listen to others and make compromises. You may need both time and encouragement from the others in your life in order to develop the "meet-you-in-the-middle" skills associated with healthy functioning within business and personal relationships.

One Power Issue: What If You Earn More Than He Does?

Perceived or actual power gives the one with the most money the larger decision-making power. That one seems to be more able to do things and buy whatever he or she wants. Also, there appears to be more authority in the richer one to decide how the money will be shared, spent, invested, and given away. Men who are romantically involved with women who earn more than they do frequently feel less respected than they should. Some are the subject of jokes from friends who assume that the woman in the relationship pays for everything. It takes a secure man to take such teasing and not allow the financial disparities to result in destructive ego-driven games within the relationship. Some men do have this kind of security, and are more than happy to allow the woman in their lives to assume a lead role in any number of areas. Others feel utterly powerless.

The woman in such a relationship is subject to some complicated feelings, too. Some of her worries have to do with the fear of sharing money with someone who isn't committed to the relationship, or with a sense of uncertainty as to her partner's true motives. The partner who brings in more money can be critical of how the other partner uses that money, ashamed of how little she herself knows about managing finances, or, as is so often the case with the Power Seeker, eager to use money and earning power as a means of control in the relationship. Some women like to "take care" of men while others hate it and want them to pull their own weight.

WHEN YOU MAKE MORE MONEY THAN HE DOES
Do:

- Plan and discuss money management before you get married. Discuss who will take care of specific financial responsibilities such as bills, the checkbook, and investments.

- Prepare for changes such as leaving work to have a family.

- Appreciate each others' skills where money is concerned; take advantage of each others' strong suits.

- Share your childhood memories about money.

- Let your partner know your worst fears and highest hopes about money.

- Tell your partner how you feel about his or her way of handling money.

- Be honest about your assets and liabilities.

Don't:

- Postpone important financial discussions.

- Encourage your man to confuse masculinity with earning power. Keep the topics separate in all your discussions.

- Marry a Power Seeker who makes a habit of shutting down the lines of communication on issues of importance to you, or attempting to control you with money or earning power. You deserve to feel power within the relationship, too.

True Power

Why is it so important to feel in control of your life? Well, think about the way you'd prefer to travel. If you have someplace to go, wouldn't you rather spend some time in the driver's seat than always be the one in the back seat? Most of us would. Why? Because when you're driving, you have the power to go where you please, as fast or as slow as you want. You can choose to pass someone or not, you can take any detours that seem attractive, and you don't have to rely on anybody else to make it to the door safely. When you sit in the back seat, on the other hand, you are dependent on the skill of the driver to get you some place in one piece. You simply don't have much say in the matter.

If your relationship sometimes places you in the driver's seat, and sometimes places you in the back seat, that relationship is one that features enough room for you to grow as an adult. If your relationship is one in which you are never, under any circumstances, in the driver's seat, there's a problem.

When you assume control of your life, you take on the role of an adult. It is often hard to be an adult because adults have to accept the consequences of their actions. You have to make decisions, and odds are that some of them will be mistakes. As an adult, you take responsibility for outcomes. If you yield responsibility for your situation to someone else— say, a Power Seeker—you give up your power to act as an adult, and you should expect to experience the deep resentment that accompanies always being told what to do.

As children, you were told what to do. Some people choose to keep on being told what to do well into adulthood, but they pay a very heavy price for that choice. They sacrifice their own growth, they don't feel particularly good about themselves, and they tend to drift through life. People who drift through life are, as a general rule, unhappy. The ones who make choices and risk having decisions come out poorly may not always win, but they do have more control—healthy control—over their lives. Not taking any risks, by contrast, is simply depressing. It gets you absolutely nowhere.

Fear and Growth

There is a degree of anxiety that accompanies being in control of one's own life, financially or otherwise. But guess what? You cannot grow without some anxiety in your life.

The good news is that when you meet your own challenges and take charge of your situation, either on your own or as an equal partner in a relationship, you will feel much greater levels of self-confidence and self-esteem. It's only when you try to buy out of the process, either by assuming no control or, as in the case of the Power Seeker, all of the control in a relationship, that things start to go wrong.

Feeling True, Nonabusive Power

How do you take constructive, healthy control of your life and your relationships? To start with, think about what is possible. So many things are out of your control that your lives can sometimes appear overwhelming and paralyzing. But they really aren't. Most of the things you worry about that are out of control don't lead to the catastrophes you're afraid they will. Check out the reality of any situation by emphasizing the available alternatives and assuming a "What can I do?" attitude. Look for your alternatives.

Talking sensibly to yourself is also extremely important. You often say things to yourself that you would never say to your worst enemy. Power Seekers certainly do this, as do the people who are trapped in relationships with them. If you fall into either category, you owe yourself a change.

Think about it. Your self put-downs are probably far harsher than any words a high-powered prosecutor could come up with. Is that really the way you want to live your life? It's possible that the verdict of "Guilty" is, all too often, the pronouncement of the judge in your own head, a pronouncement that allows no appeal and admits no plea for mercy. Fire that judge. Bring in a more fair and tolerant one. The sentence you impose on yourself needs to be reviewed. Too often we condemn ourselves for crimes that have no names. Ask yourself, "What did I do to deserve the punishment?" Does the punishment fit the crime?

You may also want to work on speaking up and asserting yourself with regard to what you feel, want, and don't want. There is no guarantee that others will change by hearing you out, but speaking up beats keeping quiet and simmering, with no chance of change. Big changes are possible. Whether it's moving, buying a house, changing jobs or careers, getting married, having children or not, divorcing or staying married, you should find an area of your life that you control and remind yourself that you do have a say in these matters. Many people, especially those victimized by long-term relationships with Power Seekers, don't realize that such changes are within their power.

Think of all the ways you can be in control of your life. You can structure your own time to avoid boredom. You can, in the final analysis, pick and choose whatever activities you wish, decide who you want to be with and for how long, and determine how much energy you're going to allot to any pursuit. You can research and choose your own investments, advisors, and financial firms. You can buy things to decorate your home, accessorize your outfits, and revitalize your lifestyle. You can decide what to eat, drink, smoke, or avoid. Finally, and perhaps most importantly, how you feel, how you react to each situation you encounter, is really under your control. You don't need anyone else's approval to decide how you will respond to any circumstance. If you're looking for someone to mother you, check the nearest mirror. That person is the perfect candidate. Depend on her for the job since she's the only one who knows what you really want.

If you have taken yourself for granted in the past, stop right now. Stop minimizing your talents, brain, and accomplishments. If you have fallen under the influence of a Power Seeker who made a habit of downplaying or belittling your talents, take some special time to yourself to send positive messages that counteract the negative ones you've received.

Attitudes can make or break you. No matter what your past experience is, no matter how painful an interaction with someone else may have been in the past, you can control how you think, how you see the world, and how you approach life in general. Instead of complaining to yourself, or lecturing yourself on the importance of avoiding mistakes, mobilize your own energy and take control. Negative attitudes drain energy. You cannot afford that, because energy is a precious commodity.

Make an effort to size up the reality of your situation; that will keep you on track. Fears and faulty assumptions blur reality. Clear up the fuzz. Feeling worried? Ask yourself, "What is the worst thing that can happen?" Usually, you'll realize that the potential outcome is not as terrifying as you think. Then ask what steps you can take to improve your own situation. What alternatives do you have? What did you do in the past when you felt in a bind? Remind yourself that you are no longer a child, but an adult. As an adult, you are under no obligation to respond to situations in old, ineffective ways.

Take a personal inventory of your own past successes. Odds are that you will realize that you can make positive changes in your life, because you have already done so. You may be amazed at the major challenges you've faced and overcome. If you've ever interviewed for a job, survived a blind date, or even followed a set of bad directions in a strange city, guess what? You've been able to tackle an intimidating situation and come out wiser and more in control.

Once again, remind yourself that having choices is the best part of taking control. It simply feels better to have alternatives than to be stuck without any clue as to what will happen next. Keeping options open, seeking alternatives, and thinking big will help you fight off any feelings of being boxed in by past problems. There is no law requiring you to continue adhering to a negative pattern, even one you may have followed for a long time. Go beyond the invisible lines you have drawn around your way of thinking. Expand on what you wish for. Reduce the layers of worry surrounding that objective.

Start Feeling True, Nonexploitative Power Right Now

Getting started on feeling truly powerful can be the most difficult part. You can overcome this problem by setting realistic expectations and goals. It really is within your power to say, "Stop the music. I will not continue to spin around in circles." Brainstorming is a way to think of alternatives. It gets you the distance you need for seeing choices and ridding yourself of worry.

Once you set aside a little time to recognize your own strengths, identify choices and alternatives, and remember that you have pulled yourself back on track in the past when things seemed overwhelming, you will be in a position to steadily increase your own self-confidence. By taking one step at a time, you can regain a sense of genuine control in your own life. You will feel better, and your relationships will improve, too.

Chapter **6**

The Freedom Searchers

Susan's Story

*S*usan *runs her own party-planning business. She was divorced once and is now widowed. She's been through a lot in life, and is happy to say that she values her freedom above everything else. She dismisses talk of long-term financial planning, instead choosing to focus on the present.*

"I'm grown-up," she explains, "and while I have a lot on my plate, I'm not going to be a child and hope that I'll be taken care of. I can take care of myself. Having money is nice . . . and being comfortable is fine, but I don't have to peg my whole life on making the money or being obsessed with what the stock market is doing each day. I can enjoy my life and find a balance in it even though I don't have a whole lot of money."

Susan may find that the balance she applauds now may be sadly lacking as she approaches her later years precisely because she is not planning for those years now.

To the Freedom Searchers like Susan, money means an escape from the everyday demands of life, including work, playing politics, and doing what others want them to do. With enough money, Freedom Searchers believe they can avoid being pushed around and be left entirely to their own devices. Unlike the Power Seekers, they're not interested in competing; in some cases, they feel too inadequate to do so. Their instinct is simply to walk away from the rat race. Sometimes, this leads to deceptive "freedoms" that only wind up imprisoning the Freedom Searchers over the long run.

You may want to take the following quiz. It will help you identify whether or not you are a Freedom Searcher. It will also give you insights into the behavior of those in your life who may fall into this category.

The Freedom Searcher's Quiz

(Answer Yes or No to the following questions.)

1. Have you balanced your checkbook within the last forty-five days?

2. Do you have a specific plan to handle the financial demands you may face ten or fifteen years from now?

3. If your employer suddenly went out of business and you had no access to unemployment funds, would you have enough savings to last you for more than a month?

4. Have you pushed one or more credit cards to the limit?

5. Do you have a strategy in place to transfer your existing skills to another industry, or develop new ones, in the event of a sudden change in your job situation?

6. Do you regularly spend money on convenience foods?

7. Do you stick to a budget?

8. Have you taken steps to combat the effects of inflation you will face when you retire?

9. Has a friend or relative ever complained to you, perhaps jokingly, about your constant tardiness or procrastination?

10. Have you had moderate to severe communication problems with such authority figures as teachers, principals, school counselors, or supervisors over the years?

Scoring

For questions 1–8, give yourself 1 point for every "yes" answer. For questions 9 and 10, give yourself 1 point for every "no" answer.

If you scored 5 or fewer points, you may be making some expensive money mistakes that are keeping you from working toward true—rather than illusory—freedom and independence.

True Financial Freedom Means Making a Plan

If you are a woman who falls into the Freedom Searcher category, you should take the time to review your outlook on financial affairs. The right to determine your own agenda, rather than the dictates of others, does not carry with it a guarantee that future events will always go your way. You should carefully consider how you will address the future obstacles you are likely to face. Bear in mind the following facts:

- Female earning power still lags significantly behind that of men.

- In the first year after a marital split, the average woman's standard of living falls 26 percent, compared to a 34 percent rise for men, according to the Women's Legal Defense Fund.

- Only 46 percent of female pre-retirees began saving for their future before age 40, versus 67 percent of the males, according to a recent Merill Lynch survey.

True freedom is not the same as rebelling against the idea of planning ahead, simply for the sake of rebelling. If you frequently have trouble addressing such innocent "consensus" questions as how to spend vacation time or where to go for dinner with friends, or if you've had to make your way through a number of jobs because you can't stand the "regimentation" of a regular schedule, it's possible that your quest for personal freedom is being conducted at too high a cost.

People who are committed to positive outcomes plan for them and find a special kind of freedom in doing so. Positively oriented people enjoy the freedom to go after what's good for them, and they can also be happy for others when they get what they want. On the other hand, people who spend most of their time being angry over the attainments of colleagues, or resentful of the control that they imagine others hold over events, are usually eager to plot ways to escape from what could turn out to be healthy relationships. These people may stage "rebellions" in the name of personal independence that backfire against themselves.

There's a paradox associated with freedom. If you are truly free, you know that you can't live life completely on your own. You develop a sense of acceptance when it comes to handling the legitimate obligations you have toward others. Many Freedom Searchers, however, deeply resent even the vaguest hint of intrusion on their autonomy, even when it comes to planning for their own futures.

Andrea

Andrea likes to think of herself as an independent person. "I hate feeling obligated to other people," she says, "and I usually insist on paying my own way. While most people network with each other to do business, I prefer not having to do favors for others. I won't allow myself any extra dependency on other people."

People like Andrea may proclaim their independence to the world by building walls around themselves, but inside they often yearn for dependence because they didn't get enough warmth, reassurance, and guidance when they were young. All the same, they deny their own desire for closeness and support, sometimes to the point of paranoia, because they fear that other people have ulterior motives and will suck them into situations from which they won't be able to escape. Since they feel the need to protect themselves from being hurt, ridiculed, or abused, Freedom Searchers focus primarily on activities they can do by themselves.

As a response to the fear of being boxed in, these people often don't own much. They rent, rather than buy, because they need to have that "footloose" feeling in their domestic arrangements. They're likely to have sparsely furnished apartments as well. Their motto is "Don't fence me in," so if you expect members of this group to stick around for long-term relationships, you're often disappointed.

Often, the Freedom Searchers' childhood was one where there was either money in abundance or virtually no money at all. In either case, money was meaningless. Too much or too litle money causes people to attach little meaning to it. To the Freedom Searcher, money is often more important as a symbol. It is something that gives you independence and choices such as whether or not to work, whether or not to stay in one place when things get complicated, and whether or not to listen when someone else has something to say.

Many extremely creative people are Freedom Searchers. They will work exceedingly hard writing books, plays, and articles. Then, they'll disappear to some remote island to be a beach bum for a season. Often, that's exactly the kind of freedom this group wants. They work when they want to, make enough headway on a project to do as they wish, and generally come and go as they please. Don't look for much of an inheritance from them either, since these are the people whose cars sport bumper stickers that proudly proclaim, "We're spending our children's inheritance."

No one really wants to consider that something bad will happen to us. You think that illness, layoffs, business setbacks, and divorce are all things that happen to other people. If you have no desire to change jobs or look at an entirely new career now, you may assume that you'll always feel this way. If you've recently gotten out of school, you may hope and pray that you'll never have to see a textbook or write a term paper again. These are understandable reactions. But smart women who want to be truly emotionally and financially independent have to take into account some of the modern-day facts of economic life. And one of those facts is that none of you can count on things always going smoothly, especially regarding money, so it's imperative to keep yourself informed about economic news and how it can affect you. You'd be wise to learn new skills that help you remain competitive in today's job market, as well as to be valued in your present one.

Remember Susan, who focuses on her current freedom? She may find herself unprepared for retirement or for a sudden financial setback.

Cheryl

Cheryl spent to her credit card maximum and then got laid off. "I never dreamed I would lose that job," she laments. "Now I'm in hot water because I have no cushion." She figured she'd be employed at her company forever, but the firm was bought out and underwent a restructuring campaign. Cheryl's ten years of experience and top-drawer salary now meant that she was too expensive to keep on the payroll.

Cheryl thought she was indispensable. She never bothered to take any computer courses or learn any special skill that might have helped her find another position within her company. In today's job market, flexibility and computer literacy are absolutely essential, but Cheryl didn't bother to think about what might happen if the needs of the company changed overnight. As anyone who's been through a downsizing campaign can attest, overnight change is a real possibility in this increasingly turbulent economy.

When Cheryl told me about her lifestyle in her pre-layoff days, I realized that the cushion she needed now had been tossed away on things like nightly take-out sprees. "I thought I'd save time by buying prepared things. Standing in a supermarket check-out line isn't my thing," she explained, none too convincingly. This "time-saving" rationalization points out the potential downside to the Freedom Searcher's approach, when that approach is taken to an extreme. Cheryl spent so much money, and saved herself so much time that she eventually found she could not make ends meet.

When you add up the cost of lunches out, taxis, housekeepers, and the like, many Freedom Searchers toss away small fortunes that should instead be committed to retirement planning. I'm not advocating giving up labor and time-saving initiatives, but I am suggesting that many of the Freedom Searchers out there could benefit from some prioritizing. What's more important, anyway—eating sushi or saving for an independent retirement?

The Budget Battle

For most of you, and especially for Freedom Searchers, the concept of having to restrain yourself financially makes spending that much more attractive. In this way, I think, working within a budget is a little like dieting. As soon as you decide to lose a few pounds, food becomes more important than ever. ("Whatever you do, don't think about a big, sticky, gooey, hot fudge sundae . . .")

Why not put the idea into a positive context? I like to think in terms of goals, rather than budgets. Once I decide that I want something, I'll definitely try to make it happen, even if I have to put up with a minor hardship along the way. With a goal-oriented approach, you can choose what you want to cut back on, and thus feel more control over the situation than you would if you were trying to live through an across-the-board deprivation. If I have to spend less on clothes shopping in order to meet a financial goal I've set for myself, so be it. I still get to rent a video every Wednesday night and go out for dinner on the weekend. I've made the choices.

Small savings add up. The trick, especially if you're a Freedom Searcher, is to start making those small savings happen. Women who procrastinate when it comes to saving money are hurting themselves when they don't take advantage of, for example, compounding interest or rising stock prices. Even if the amounts of money involved seem modest at first, you should still act now. As I pointed out earlier in this chapter, the average woman's earning power in this society is still significantly less than the average man's. As of this writing, that discrepancy is reflected in an overall pay rate of 72 cents for every dollar a man earns.

It's quite understandable that women have more trouble saving than men do since they earn less. This is, nevertheless, an obstacle you must focus your energies on overcoming, particularly if your instinctive pattern is that of a Freedom Searcher. For specific advice on a savings and investment plan that's appropriate to your situation, you should meet with a qualified investment advisor. Don't postpone making the appointment. By meeting with an experienced financial professional, you'll be increasing your options for the future, and this in turn will provide you with greater autonomy as you grow older.

Dana and Nick

Dana and Nick aren't married, but they're definitely a couple. They're both divorced; each has children from prior marriages, and each describes their relationship as a "perpetual honeymoon." For eight years, they've lived separately but get together often for intimacy, fun, and companionship. Dana and Nick call themselves "apartners."

Both of them had to struggle to extract themselves from past commitments. Dana wanted desperately to establish her own identity, one that was separate from the roles of wife and mother that she found suffocating. "I got sick and tired of thinking of 'we,' and needed to think of 'me'," she told me. "If I lived with Nick, I'd be stuck again having to ask him for permission to do things, as I did with my ex. I'm just finding out who I am and what I like to do, and I'm not willing to give that up by living with Nick."

Nick's need for independence was somewhat different. He was ready to define himself in a way that transcended the demands of his past family responsibilities. He fulfilled his obligation as father and husband for twenty years and vowed that he'd "never again be responsible for anyone's health and happiness." Nick felt that he wanted to avoid relationships that "drained him of his time, energy, and finances."

Dana and Nick, both Freedom Searchers, found that living apart, while considering each other the "favorite partner," was a workable solution to a series of complex problems. Their unusual living arrangement allows each of them to feel autonomous and independent while still being involved. They maintain responsibility for their own lives. When they are alone, they each feel comfortable and in control. They miss each other when they're apart, but they enjoy being by themselves, too. They avoid the daily domestic frustrations that proved crippling in their past relationships. They don't take each other for granted, nor do they fight. Both boast about the advantages of being involved in a romance that is kept alive by not seeing each other every day. Dana and Nick also claim that their sex life together has benefited tremendously from the eager anticipation that is a regular part of their relationship.

Dana and Nick have set up their financial arrangement to reflect their shared desire for equality. "I want to avoid all those issues of control and dependency," Dana explains. "One takes over and the other has to follow. I did that in my marriage, and I won't do it again. Living apart helps to equalize the playing field." That's why they split expenses down the middle. When they go on vacation, they keep a record of "His," "Hers," and "Ours" expenses. Other couples with sizable income differences may opt to divide things differently. Often, the one with the larger income pays for things like dinners and vacations. As the pay increases for the one with the lower income, his or her expenses rise incrementally, as well.

The independence these "apartners" crave is also applied to their households. Each is responsible for their own and their respective children's expenses at home. Dana and Nick have found that love and caring for each other is not contingent on financial attachment. By helping each other through crises, offering companionship and intimacy, and then going home to their own domestic situations, they maintain their hard-won freedom. For the Freedom Searcher, such an arrangement may offer the best of both marriage and single life.

Dana and Nick's solution may not work for everyone, (particularly if you have younger children who still live with you) but it is certainly an option worth considering if you are a Freedom Searcher who wants to maintain your hard-won freedom and have the best that marriage offers without the pitfalls.

"Take Care of Me"

Freedom poses a problem for many women. Often it means having choices, going places alone, tackling unfaced challenges, meeting responsibilities for the first time, learning new things, and meeting different people. For generations, women were programmed to, first and foremost, seek security in their relationships with men. Today, many women have concluded that marriage and commitment are no longer synonymous with a willingness to "stand behind" a man and define themselves through his accomplishments.

True freedom can be frightening because it means exploring your own values, expressing your own opinions, and being true to one's self. You need not follow a parent's or husband's way of thinking or doing things. The separation from the familiar into the unknown takes courage, and it often takes time, too.

In childhood, both boys and girls learn dependency. Young children expect to be nurtured, cared for, and protected. You are encouraged, as a child, to lean on someone stronger than yourself. Although boys are conditioned early on to move beyond dependent childhood relationships as they enter young adulthood, girls very often are not. For some women, the process of establishing a healthy sense of autonomy is a lifelong process, one that is very likely to be marked by setback after setback. Among the obstacles may be the instinct to be "saved" by a man, whether financially or in other ways. Such desires are often deeply rooted in early social conditioning.

Many women struggle long and hard to come to terms with the idea of freedom. Freedom and autonomy—associated with mature, foresighted, and responsible adults—may carry a stigma for those who have been trained to look at themselves as wives and mothers, period. All too often, women have been conditioned to believe that self-sufficiency simply isn't feminine, or that it is inconsistent with women's responsibilities to others. It is very easy indeed to fall into the "nurturer" or "serving" roles women have been encouraged to perform for centuries, and to ignore or downplay your own talents and interests in the process.

Although some Freedom Searching women, eager to escape this brand of stereotyping, short-change themselves when it comes to taking meaningful responsibility for the future, their initial instincts are quite sound. It makes sense to stand up for your own right to define yourself and your interests. Where the Freedom Searcher often goes astray, of course, is in seeing any form of planning as inherently restrictive to personal freedom.

Karen and Debby

Karen was married for twenty years to a man she helped through graduate school. Although she had an I.Q. of 145 and a strong aptitude for the sciences, Karen worked as a secretary to help her husband pursue his own educational goals. After she had had three children, and her husband's career had gone into overdrive, Karen learned that her partner was leaving.

He told her she was boring and that she was incapable of holding meaningful conversations. Then, he was gone. What was she to do? She was unskilled, overweight, scared to death, and forty years old. Starting over from such a point in one's life certainly isn't impossible, but it can certainly seem intimidating at first.

Compare Karen's story to Debby's. Debby left her job when her first child was born. For the next ten years, she took courses in psychology and eventually got her Ph.D. When she and her husband decided to call it quits, she flourished. She welcomed having her own apartment, friends, and assorted lovers. She worked part-time and developed a small private practice that developed slowly but steadily. She spent time planning for her own future, but she refused to indulge in undue anxiety over how she'd manage her life, career, and finances. In other words, she showed balance and a sense of perspective in assessing her future goals without compromising her own outlook as a Freedom Searcher.

Because she believed in herself and her ability to pursue her endeavors, Debby was unconflicted about being free. There was no angst over her femininity and there was no self-doubt about her resourcefulness and other personal assets. Her attitude was, "If I could get a Ph.D., I can do anything." She'll admit to having intermittent yearnings for dependency, but she'll then remind herself that she's perfectly capable of taking the best possible care of herself.

Often, it is the therapist's job to help women like Karen become more like Debby. The process starts with an awareness that something has to change. Depression, anxiety, physical problems, and panicky feelings are the usual symptoms. An inability to move forward to do something to feel better makes people angry at themselves—and keeps them on the fence.

The internal conflict usually sounds like this: "If I do A, B will be lost. If I do C, somebody I love might be hurt. If I do nothing, I hurt myself." There are no positive outcomes in such oft-replayed stories. Discovering exactly what will be lost, who may or may not be hurt, and what life would really be like with more independence and less dependence, can be an eye-opening experience. Many women find that what they stand to lose isn't worth holding on to in the first place.

Is there something you're afraid of losing that isn't even worth the time and effort you're spending worrying about it? Discussing who may be hurt by your independence will sound bizarre once you explore all your negative fantasies in detail. They will be exposed for the mirages they are if only you take the time to examine them objectively.

Envisioning how life can be with freedom and independence generally lifts the weight of depression. Getting out from under the victim stance—where "they" seem to have power over you—is vitally important. No one else can do that. It's you who are holding yourself back through your own fears. Make a commitment to look at your fears related to failure, success, new experiences, and aging. Talk them over with a therapist or close friend. Once you do, you'll be in a better position to experience true freedom in your life.

Your attitudes—the ways you think about things, people, and events—may need to be fine-tuned. You may be surprised to learn how often you perceive things in black-and-white terms. "All or nothing" is an extremist attitude, one to which Freedom Searchers often adhere to with less than stellar results. Instead, you should think about doing well enough.

Do ideas like these sound familiar?

"If I had more money, I'd manage it better."

"I just don't have much of a head for figures. If I don't meet the right guy within the next few years, then I'll start thinking about retirement."

"It's better for me to stay on my own now, because I'd probably screw up any relationship I stumbled into."

These are classic Freedom Searcher dodges. Rationalizing and denying are just tricks that protect you from the reality of being free. The truth is that you are neither so perfect as to have all the answers, nor are you such a zero as to be unworthy of any happiness. The truth is in the middle. You've got to replace these negative thoughts with positive self-talk, as Debby did:

"I'm a quick study; I know I can learn to handle my money intelligently."

"Knowing what my own retirement will look like is part of being confident, and confidence is incredibly attractive."

"I know how to pick out the right relationship for myself, no matter what's happened in the past."

If you are a Freedom Searcher, you will probably find the process of shedding restrictive behavior and thoughts a pleasant and exhilarating one. In time, you will learn that there is no reason to keep your secret wishes for dependency alive, and you will learn to truly rely on yourself. You'll be surprised at the energy and strength you'll have when you assume responsibility for your own problems and seek out your own alternatives. Before long, you'll be in the habit of identifying your own solutions in advance and moving forward.

If you are truly free, you'll embrace the future, rather than try to distract yourself from seeing it. You will feel:

Realistic

Grounded

Spontaneous

Released from immobility

Energized

Playful

Secure in your own identity

Secure in your own choices

Loved for your own unique qualities

Able to move toward your goals without fear

Good about setting goals

Confident

Aware of both your assets and your limitations

Unafraid to try new things

Able to believe in yourself

Self-loving

Able to love others

Start talking yourself up now. Make the move toward true freedom!

Part III

Money and the Opposite Sex

Chapter 7

Couple Talk, Money Talk

art didn't bother talking to Faye before he purchased the camel-hair winter coat at Bloomingdale's he'd had his eye on. He figured that he had put the purchase off for close to seven years— longer, he reasoned, than he had even been married *to Faye—and now the coat that was exactly what he was looking for was on sale. He'd made do with what he had for long enough. When he brought the coat home, he found he had some explaining to do.*

"How could you make a purchase like that without talking to me?" Faye wanted to know.

"I wanted it. It was a purchase that made sense. I'd been putting this off for years, and it was on sale."

"What happened," Faye asked, "to our idea of holding off on big purchases this year so we could pay off the bills we have already—and go off on that long weekend?"

"Well," Bart answered, "we'll pay it off a little each month and cut back on something else. Look, this is no big deal."

"Will it be a big deal when it happens next time?" Faye got no answer to her question. So she fired one last shot. "No big deal. We'll cut back somewhere else. You know, that's the sort of thing my dad always said to my mom right before they had a problem with the next month's rent."

There's a lot going on in this argument: power struggles, battles for priorities, fantasy fulfillment, background influences, parental issues, and, last but not least, clashing money-maintenance styles. Each partner is following an internal voice that's passing along important value-related cues, and the expression of these cues can have a major impact on each partner's sense of self-esteem and happiness within the relationship.

Bart's internal voice is saying things like:

- "I worked hard for the money. Why can't I spend it if it makes sense?"

- "Do I have to check with her before I do *everything?*"

- "It's not like I didn't think about the purchase for a good long while before making it."

Faye's internal voice is saying things like:

- "He's not remembering what we decided to do. He's dismissing our goals again on his own. That's not what being married is about."

- "He's dismissing me."

- I'd *love* to have a fur coat, but I wouldn't head out and buy it for myself. I'd drop a few broad hints. I might even tell him where to find the best deal. But I wouldn't make the decision unilaterally."

Many long-term male/female relationships—perhaps the majority of them—must come to terms with arguments along the lines of the one Bart and Faye had. Often, you must reconcile yourself to the fact that the core issues underlying the conflict must be *managed*, not resolved conclusively. Expecting an outcome in which one partner is clearly "right" and the other is clearly "wrong" may sometimes be asking too much.

Regardless of the predominant money style we follow, there are often significant barriers incorporating that style with our mate's. Many men are uncomfortable consulting with their partners when it comes to financial matters. For many women, doing so is almost second nature.

The Money and Mates Quiz

Take this test with your partner, marking your answers on a separate sheet of paper. Then review your answers according to the key that appears after the text.

1. It's your anniversary and you and your mate are dining out with another couple in an expensive restaurant, and it's their treat. Both of the people taking you out are old friends who have recently started dating. When the check arrives, the woman with whom you're double-dating picks it up. Her date seems uncomfortable. Which of the following actions would you most likely take if you were in his position?

    a) Firmly ask for the check.

    b) Shift around in your chair for a moment or two, then offer to pay the tip.

    c) Smile and mention that you'll pay for dinner next time.

    d) Make no mention of the check whatsoever, and silently conclude that your date must really like you.

2. You are a serious tennis fanatic. You know your mate is trying to save for a vacation this year, but you just saw your dream tennis racquet, marked down to $350 from $600. The sale ends today. Which of the following actions would you most likely take?

    a) Dip into the money market account and buy the racquet.

    b) Walk away from the sale, repeating the mantra-like phrase "Don't buy it, don't even think of buying it. Don't buy it, don't even think of buying it."

    c) Find some way to consult with your partner before the sale ends, no matter what it takes.

    d) Buy the racquet but fib about exactly how much it cost.

3. You're part of a two-career couple. Each of you is excited about your respective career. One day, you return from work and learn that

your partner has been offered a spectacular position with a huge salary. There is a catch. The firm is located 1,500 miles away, in a city where the cost of living is substantially lower than where you now live. Which of the following options reflects your most likely reaction to this situation?

a) Since there's all that extra money to go around, you conclude, you can now afford a bicoastal lifestyle. You urge your mate to accept the offer, and explain that you can keep your own position. The two of you can connect on the weekends.

b) Explain that you're willing to move on two conditions: the new job represents guaranteed long-term financial security *and* the new employer pays all moving expenses.

c) Try to explore, in an optimistic way, the risks and opportunities you both face, and determine how willing your partner is to consider maintaining the status quo rather than accepting the new job. Then follow whatever approach seems to make the most sense for both of you.

d) Agree to move immediately without having an in-depth discussion because you don't want your partner to think you're trying to keep him or her from earning more money.

4. You are the sole breadwinner in a relationship. Your partner wants to contribute to a nonprofit cause which you don't support. Which of these options best reflects your response to this situation?

a) Tell your partner you simply refuse to donate money to the cause.

b) Agree to give the money, primarily because you don't mind the tax deduction.

c) Agree to give the money, primarily because you know that people have different philosophies in life.

d) Agree to give the money, primarily because you don't want your partner to think you're unwilling to support him or her.

5. Your mate buys you a lottery ticket and gives it to you as a gag gift. The ticket ends up being a winner and you win $500. Which of the following would you most likely do?

a) Splurge and spend it on yourself.

b) Use the money to pay bills.

c) Spend half on yourself and give the rest to your partner so he or she can have something special, too.

d) Tell your partner he or she can choose to spend the money however he or she sees fit, on the theory that this will encourage your mate to appreciate you more.

6. Your parents recently passed away. At the reading of the will, you learn that their estate is being held in trust for you. You get a modest interest income, but the principal will eventually go to your children. Which of the following sentiments would most accurately express your reaction?

a) "They wanted to show who's boss, and they took the opportunity to do it."

b) "Great! A little extra income for us, and we don't have to worry about the kids."

c) "I didn't want anything from them anyway, so it's no big deal."

d) "This is awful. They must not have cared about me much."

7. When you met your partner, you had a number of investments, some of which your mate did not know about. Which of the following would you be most comfortable doing?

a) Keeping as much of your financial information as possible to yourself.

b) Keeping a couple of accounts secret and separate in case of an emergency.

c) Telling your mate in detail about all aspects of your finances, and addressing financial issues as equal partners.

    d) Keeping a couple of accounts secret and separate so you can spring a surprise such as a new car or a fancy vacation on your mate, thereby improving things in the relationship when the situation demands.

8. You're planning to give up your apartment to move into your partner's apartment. You're ready to have your first discussion about how you'll contribute to the joint household expenses. Which of the following approaches would you choose?

    a) Divide expenses proportionate to your relative incomes.

    b) Contribute only to those additional expenses caused by your living in the apartment.

    c) Split everything 50/50 and not worry about who earns more or less.

    d) Suggest that, if your mate is truly concerned about making the relationship work, he or she will find a way to redecorate the apartment to your liking before you discuss financial arrangements.

9. You and your spouse want to buy a computer, but money is tight. Which of the following options appeals to you most?

    a) Buy top-of-the-line and finance everything, since quality counts for something, and a good computer is an essential these days.

    b) Research extensively over a period of two months or so, and save until you find the best option in your price range at that time.

    c) Buy a second-hand computer and splurge on the software for it.

    d) Agree to buy a machine that meets your basic requirements, but make your spouse promise to allow you to upgrade it within a certain time frame, regardless of what your finances are at that point.

10. Which of the following statements best describes your philosophy when it comes to exchanging gifts with your partner on birthdays and holidays?

   a) Set a clear dollar limit.

   b) Agree to save money, rather than exchange gifts, in order to make a future purchase or payment that will benefit you both.

   c) Set a broad range that identifies what you are each willing to spend, but allow the person a certain amount of leeway within that range.

   d) Drop broad hints about gifts that your mate really ought to find some way to track down and, when you can, identify similarly expensive gifts for your mate so that he or she will know how much you care.

Scoring

If you answered most questions with an "a" response, you are probably a Power Seeker. Such things as winning, being the decision maker, and having veto power are in all likelihood quite important to you. You don't want to be taken advantage of, and you often push for your own way when you have a say in the matter. Control is a major issue for you, and you generally feel most comfortable when you have it. Keeping the occasional secret, having immediate access to important information, and identifying exactly what you want from a situation are all approaches with which you feel comfortable. You feel that quality matters, and you have a natural attraction to the best when it comes to name-brand goods.

If you answered "b" to most of the questions, you are probably a Keeper. Given the choice, it's a good bet you'd prefer to bargain, barter, or borrow before paying good money for something. The more money you can hold onto, the better you feel, even if that means temporary inconvenience. You like to think "in the long term." You probably draw a deep sigh of relief when you can assure yourself that the bills are all paid and there's something left in the bank and you consider that a real accomplishment. People may occasionally bandy about words like "penny-pinching" and "cheap," but you prefer to think of your no-frills approach as pragmatic and disciplined. When you know your money is safe, you sleep better.

If you answered "c" to most of the questions you are probably best described as a Freedom Searcher. Your preference is to take an easygoing approach to financial affairs, and you don't think getting worked up over money makes for better decisions. As a general rule, you believe that if you make intelligent choices on an ad hoc basis, things will probably turn out for the best. You have an optimistic viewpoint on most matters, including discussions of money, and you realize that people often disagree on important issues. If your mate feels strongly one way or another about a financial question, you will certainly be willing to provide intelligent observations on the situation, but you are unlikely to have a high "stake" in the issue one way or the other. It's likely that you take a "two-heads-are-better-than-one" approach to pressing financial questions, and that you have a fairly high level of trust in the answers that collaborative decision making will provide.

If you answered "d" to most of the questions above, you may be linking love, approval, and self-esteem with material things, and you may be doing so to a degree that may cause problems in your personal relationships. If you fall into this category, you may be what I call a Love Buyer, and you may be in for an unpleasant series of experiences. Expensive dinners and quality clothing are nice to have, but you should work to change your outlook on money and status, because the *amount of money spent really has nothing to do with how much someone is loved.* Even spending more money than you want to or can afford on someone does not really make someone like or appreciate you for who you truly are. Instead of tying purchase issues to your self-esteem, you may need to work toward developing a caring, open-minded attitude toward financial issues, one that clearly separates personal worth from prices, products, and expenditures.

There Are Types and There Are Types

Most of you predominantly follow *one* of the styles just outlined. You may follow it strongly or with a less pronounced emphasis than other people, but you nevertheless have a first instinct, when it comes time to assess financial questions, that falls into one of these patterns.

Of course, it's not uncommon for life-partners to be "odd couples" in how they handle money. Identifying your styles may help you understand why your mate reacts to you in the way he or she does. If you are accused of being

- Too "tight" when it comes to money

- Too "paranoid" when it comes to money

- Too "laid back" when it comes to money

- Too "impulsive and demanding" when it comes to money

. . . then there's a strong likelihood that your partner does not share your particular mindset, and is describing only the most obvious, potentially negative aspects of your personal style when it comes to dealing with financial issues. These pronouncements are not right or wrong in themselves, but simply a reflection of how your mate—who has a personal style, too—views your habits.

Typically, you look to your mate to complement your personality by providing some talent or aptitude that you seem to lack. In dealing with financial issues, however, it's a rare couple that doesn't feature partners who fight over what each perceives to be the "right" way to do things. Where fights over money are concerned, there are often hidden agendas and unmet needs—needs corresponding to the four outlooks you've just learned about—that loom far larger in importance than the actual dollars and cents of a particular purchase, investment, or strategy decision. Let's use some of the examples from the quiz to take a look at some of these issues.

Autonomy

Today, women are likely to express their personal and financial autonomy in social and relationship settings by picking up checks, setting up separate bank accounts, or developing personalized investment portfolio strategies. A certain degree of balance and perspective from *both* partners is essential in sorting through the autonomy issues women, especially professional women, must work through with their partners.

Men must understand that the desire not to be *possessed* in some abstract sense is a valid and unassailable aim on the part of contemporary women. Women must understand that many men view the degree of financial control they are capable of exerting as a measure of their worth and value. Some men are simply unwilling to assume what they view as a dependent or childlike position and will engage in seemingly pointless scrimmages over such things as the right to pick up a check at a restaurant. Remember too that men have been the providers over the centuries, and they still make more money than women.

Many women must learn, over a period of time, to develop their own personal and financial autonomy. Many men must learn, over a period of time, not to feel personally threatened by that autonomy. They are used to acting unilaterally, rather than as part of a group, in part because they are, very early in life, encouraged to perform independently and thereby attain ranks within male-oriented hierarchies. For men, who are typically socialized to separate early from their mothers and look to their fathers for guidance, the idea of "letting a woman tell me what to do" may take some getting used to. As a very general rule, though, women are trying less to tell men what to do and trying more to establish the right to make their *own* decisions on issues that affect them.

Understanding the bedrock needs your partner is showing is probably the first step toward identifying a constructive way to express autonomy-related requirements from the relationship. Open discussion of these needs is the first step toward making sense of conflicting personal and financial aims you may be experiencing in your relationship.

Decision-Making Power

Even when there is agreement on major financial goals such as the need to plan for a vacation, it's a good idea to have money available for each partner to spend without having the onus to "clear things first" with a mate. Agreeing on *how the big decisions are going to be made* matters more than the specifics of *every* spending decision.

Some people are "today" spenders; others are "tomorrow" spenders. By recognizing each other's decision-making behaviors, and strategizing some mutually acceptable middle path, such as discussing purchases over a certain amount, partners can avoid many of the heated discussions associated with spending patterns one partner cannot believe are problematic for another. You can't eliminate the difference in your outlooks but you *can* eliminate the vague "operating rules" governing those outlooks, and replace them with some considerate guidelines.

To some people, it seems impossible to save for a distant future—there's so much living to be done right now! When a Keeper is married to a Love Buyer, this conflict can become a constant—and potentially debilitating—problem for the relationship. Resolving these issues successfully is usually, but not always, a matter of allowing one partner to take the "lead role" in dealing with the important financial issues that arise on a day-to-day basis, and establishing workable ground rules that will help keep the "background" partner from feeling entirely powerless. As in so many aspects of a healthy long-term relationship, balance and tact count for a great deal.

If Love Buyers are not always the best long-term planners when it comes to a couple's financial situation, Power Seekers can run the risk of being more than a little intimidating in their efforts to maintain control of the situation. Their anger at being questioned about finances, or having a partner "go around" them, can be impressive enough to keep others submissive during discussions about money. Sometimes this results in blind compliance with every fiat the Power Seeker issues; sometimes it doesn't. In all too many cases, the Power Seeker encourages precisely the lack of control he or she seeks to avoid when partners decide to rebel by stashing money away secretly, skimming from budgets, and snitching from wallets and bureau tops. Often, when a partner insists on getting educated or taking a paying job, the relationship ends.

Risk-Taking

As a general principle, men and women experience financial risks, such as those associated with the decision to leave one job and move to take on another, in very different ways. Although a larger salary may represent more security, power, and freedom to members of both sexes, many women will show strong concern for "roots," related issues affecting relationships with friends and family, issues that aren't as important for men. Of critical importance, of course, is a woman's relationship with her mate. This factor may be and often is the deciding factor in favor of a decision to leave one's own job so that a husband may take on a new assignment.

A man, on the other hand, is more likely to *define himself* in terms of his job. He is also, as a very general rule, more likely to take risks than a woman in part because of his socialization. Typically, as they grow up, men are rewarded for undertaking bold new initiatives or for successfully seeing through a confrontation with another man. The pressure to "provide" may be more likely to encourage a man to take a course of action, or a series of courses of action, that most women would shy away from. By contrast, young girls are very often socialized to exhibit extreme caution in their interactions with others by, for instance, not staying out after dark, and by emphasizing neatness and cleanliness as a means of controlling the way others perceive them.

The bottom line: as a broad principle, men tend to see risk as a series of 50/50 propositions, and may not think much of pursuing a succession of risks, often with little or no preparation or debate, in order to attain an important goal. Women, on the other hand, are far likelier to require a period of reasoned *discussion, assessment,* and *strategizing* before committing to a risky undertaking. Understanding and accounting for these dynamics will go a long way toward reducing the stress you and your mate experience when you're discussing financial issues. Men may want to consider incorporating more "debate" into their financial discussions than might be their first instinct, while women may want to remind themselves that trying to examine *all* the possible ramifications of a financial decision, even an important one, may be counterproductive.

Investing Differences

Secrets are hard to keep. Even squirreling away your assets from the prying eyes of your mate, as one of the responses in the quiz permitted you to do, doesn't free you from the dictates of Uncle Sam, who likes to know about *all* your income! (By the way, a wise spouse will refuse to sign a tax return without understanding it. When in doubt, he or she will ask for explanations and inquire about the accounts where interest are is declared.)

In addition to being difficult to maintain, secrets have a habit of eroding relationships. Trust is fundamental to a good partnership, and that extends to financial matters. Some people who have a lot of money don't want others to know about it, for fear that the financial issues will color the relationship. Initially, they may downplay their income status, because they have an understandable desire to be liked for something other than their money. This approach may make a certain amount of sense during the early stages of a relationship, but it's no way to run a marriage or a lifelong partnership.

Don't assume that any money you bring to a marriage remains yours. State law varies and in some locales, any property you bring to a marriage becomes marital property. In fact, if you have a substantial amount of money or property, you should consult an attorney and discuss ways to protect these assets in the event your marriage breaks up.

It's a good idea to have your own money available for an emergency, and you don't have to keep this a secret. You and your mate can plan for this together. I recommend separate accounts for discretionary funds, too.

Many women defer financial matters to their husbands by assuming that their mates know a lot more about financial matters than they do. This feeds into their desire to be taken care of—a nice thought, but not at all smart. Guess what? Very often, men don't know much about money management. Many a disastrous cycle of cover-up and deception has arisen because of man's ill-conceived attempts to rectify or conceal his own incompetence with regard to financial matters. The fact that men are "supposed" to know how to handle money often serves as a significant disincentive for men to ask their mates for the help and perspective they need. It also keeps women in the dark and dependent about the financial facts of life. Too many widows wish they knew what the financial realities were before their husband's death. Adjustment to this stage of life is hard enough without having to learn the basics of money management.

Women are, as a general rule, more likely than men to gather significant amounts of data before pursuing a particular investment strategy. They are also likelier to blame themselves for a stock's poor performance, and give credit to the person who helped them select the stock when it does well. Men, by contrast, are likelier to take credit for their own successful investments, and place blame on the broker or company who sold them a stock that did not do well. They are also more likely to say their friend from the golf club who gave them a hot tip is the one to blame if the investment goes sour. Women also tend to be more wary of the "big killing" investment than men, preferring to put small sums of money in safe places and leave the money alone for long periods.

Incorporating these differences in perspective into your assessments of your investment plan will not only promote domestic harmony; it may lead to a valuable discussion of basic investment objectives, a step too many couples overlook.

Conflicting Needs

When a couple decides to make a major purchase, the agreement between the partners may end there. Consider the computer purchase discussed in the quiz. A Keeper or a Freedom Searcher will probably be happy with the bare-bones approach, and may be content to save or buy a second-hand model. A Power Seeker or a Love Buyer, on the other hand, will want to find some way to get the model with the latest bells and whistles as quickly as possible. Finding a workable compromise may require members of each group to make a little healthy movement toward the center.

In addressing conflicts in these areas, it may also be helpful to bear in mind that men and women often view product purchases very differently. For a man, a computer may be a status symbol, something that earns him respect within a certain hierarchy. The laptop must not only accomplish a certain list of tasks, but elicit *admiration* and *respect* from those with whom he comes into contact. Women are more concerned with *cooperation* and *a sense of being liked*, rather than establishing a dominant position or competing. They'll buy things to get compliments or to get a job done.

Gift Shopping

Gifts say a lot about a relationship as we saw in the question that dealt with this issue in the quiz.

An important note for both men and women: Sometimes gifts are offered as a substitute for true communication. Often, a pricey gift says, in essence, "I'm sorry. Forgive me. Let's make up." By spending a substantial sum of money, you may come off as Santa Claus, but are you also keeping your feelings of disappointment and resentment to yourself?

Expensive gifts may also be Power Seeker maneuvers. Someone who gives "the really good stuff" may be saying, in so many words, "You do as I say, and I'll take care of you. Continue to please me, and I'll continue to reward you." This approach may be dazzling at first, but it's not the stuff of which solid partnerships are made. Mutuality and shared values are more important than big price tags.

Power Seekers, especially those who are males, have also been known to give "controlling" gifts. These are gifts that reflect the giver's interests and concerns, not the recipient's. They are essentially gifts that say either "stay in your place" as with household appliances and kitchenware or "follow me" as in the case of golf clubs and tennis racquets presented to a mate, who does not pursue those sports. These gifts are usually given by an enthusiast who feels a little guilty about the time he spends away from home. These gifts, almost universally given to women by men rather than the other way around, are rarely seen as inappropriate by the givers.

Love Buyers often fall into gift-related traps, as well. A patient of mine was so used to receiving expensive jewelry from her husband that she was unable to admit the possibility of any positive sentiment in a gift he picked up from a street peddler—an attractive hand-made, artsy black-and-white plastic barrette. She was furious. After a year of therapy, this woman was finally able to admit that the gift had less to do with her husband's love for her and more to do with the fact that he had suffered financial setbacks since his last round of gift-giving. She came to the point where she was able to laugh with him about her initial reaction and say, "Well, do you remember the days of wine and roses, when you gave me sterling silver? Look how far we've come. And we're still together, right?"

MONEY TALK: SOME GROUND RULES

- Accept that talking about differences in your styles is better than not talking about the differences.

- Accept that there is no right or wrong way to deal with financial issues.

- If you confuse the price of things you're given with how much you are loved, you are unrealistic and need to have a more mature way to react to others' gifts.

- If you're too tight with money, make an effort to loosen up.

- If you're too loose, make an effort to show more discipline.

Women: Remember that men react poorly to being told how to act. Come up with better ways to get your ideas across. Nobody likes to be told what to do, even you, right? Stick to positives with lots of appreciation.

Men: Remember that women may need more time to analyze situations and choices that may seem to you to be absolutely necessary. Don't fight this. Strive to point it in the right direction and don't be afraid to get a head start on an important financial objective by doing some of the homework yourself.

Men and Women: Talk and listen. Understanding your partner's money behavior and opinions can help you create peace instead of World War III.

Chapter 8

He Said, She Said: Addressing the Most Serious Money Conflicts in Committed Relationships

*J*udy *and Steve were about to get married and wanted to buy a personal computer. She used it mostly for word processing, while Steve was eager to set up a system to keep track of personal expenses for tax purposes.*

The longer they looked around for the right package, the more involved Steve got in researching the details of the purchase. Which software offered the best features? Which monitor had the sharpest, crispest image? Which printer was fastest? Judy, on the other hand, simply wanted something that would allow her to keep her correspondence in order. She was eager to find something inexpensive, even if that meant making do with an ancient software program. "Steve wanted a Cadillac computer and I wanted a Jeep," Judy observed.

What might have turned into a power struggle over high-tech priorities became an enlightening discussion about the hidden needs behind each partner's objective. First and foremost, Judy wanted to save money, and thought she deserved a medal for her efforts. Steve wanted to stake out his place in the technological revolution, and, perhaps just as importantly, he wanted to "be able to talk with the other guys." He gloated over the prospect of one-upping his buddies by boasting about all the extra features that his computer had that theirs did not.

Some people, such as Steve, want the best that money can buy—not necessarily in order to fulfill a particular purpose—but as a symbol of their own status. Quality, often represented by something that will impress another person, is the most important objective. Toys such as CD players, photography equipment, cars, and computers often capture the male imagination because of their promises of speed, durability, reliability, and power, as well as the implied advantages of these benefits. One of the major advantages, of course, is being able to boast about the new purchase.

Economically empowered women are also likely to want these fancy high-tech toys but they may approach the purchase from an entirely different perspective. Usually, the attitude behind a woman's purchase of one of these status items is likely to be, "I deserve this," or, "This is a practical purchase," or, "I can save money with this." The man, on the other hand, may be thinking, "This is something that will show others how far I've climbed on the ladder of success."

For some couples, a dispute such as Steve and Judy's computer search can be long and bitter indeed. One partner may insist on the virtues of the low-budget approach. The other may hold out for the right to make a purchase that carries what appear to be important social implications, but may never openly discuss these implications. In addressing the deeper issues, you may be able to work out a compromise more quickly and smoothly. For Judy and Steve, the compromise took the form of a reconditioned computer with a newly installed high-speed modem. This option gave Steve some measure of pride in his purchase while letting Judy feel she had gotten good value for the money spent.

Resolving Fights Over Money

Although money disputes don't cause all couples to split up, it's fair to say that in virtually every committed relationship, there will be serious conflicts about money. Trying to follow some guidelines to resolve these money fights can be helpful.

Think of dealing with money disputes within a serious relationship as a three-part challenge. Together, you will both try to

1. Identify and discuss your differences.

2. Identify the things you both agree on.

3. Strategize ways to attain common goals.

These steps may sound simple enough, but trust me, in practice they can be quite challenging!

To establish a calm and productive atmosphere for a discussion, agree ahead of time that it's in both your interests to resolve your differences. You'll need to set aside a special time so you won't be distracted or rushed. Here are some ground rules to follow:

1. Only one person may talk at a time

2. No interrupting or ridiculing

3. No attacking

4. No yelling

5. Each partner should make an effort not to criticize or maintain a negative, closed-minded attitude

If you and your partner are both committed to following these guidelines, you'll be in a better position to benefit from a positive discussion. If, however, things deteriorate during your conversation and you suspect that you'll be hearing your words thrown back at you at some future time, it's time to call a time-out.

Even if you don't get too far in your first attempts, don't be discouraged. Remember, the patterns that you're trying to identify and in some cases, undo, took years to develop. It will take time to change, and time for you to master the art of *really* hearing each other out.

Use what you know about your respective family backgrounds to remind each other of your "first-instinct" ways of analyzing facts or doing things. Ask yourself whether your way of looking at the current problem is similar to the way your mother or father would have done it. How did that approach work out for your parents? Is this outlook or behavior something you want to incorporate in your own life?

As a member of your own family, you must develop your own ways of dealing with money. It's similar to the attitudinal transition between "me" and "we" that newlyweds have to make in order to feel like a partnership. "My way" has to turn into "our way."

Once you start to share your underlying worries, you will find out important information about each other. The usual concerns about not having enough security, status, love, or freedom will surface eventually. In most cases, once you put these thoughts into words, you'll be able to see whether they are realistic or not.

Therapists frequently ask, "What's the worst thing that could happen?" This is a good question to bear in mind as you explore, as a committed couple, what guides each of your feelings about money. Answering this question means bringing your scariest fantasy out into the open so that it can be heard in all its ridiculousness. Fears of bankruptcy, insurmountable loss, and unbearable vulnerability are just a few of the crippling financial fantasies I've heard. "How possible is it that the worst thing you come up with could actually happen?" is another question that can put fear into perspective. The simple act of verbalizing the nightmare scenario can be liberating. You might even find yourself laughing at your own worst-case scenario. That's good!

Next, you should try to talk about your wants and wishes. It's important that you express these notions as wishes, rather than commands. This part of the process is more fun than hashing out the worries and it also helps you and your partner to feel closer. When each of you knows what the other person dreams of, you can put the fears behind you and start working to make the dreams come true. Without finding out what's important to your partner, you're just floundering and guessing what he or she really wants. I want mink earmuffs for my birthday, but if I don't speak up, no one will know this. The chances of me getting them, or anything else on my list, are better if I speak up. If you really want a house in the suburbs, say so. You may find that your partner wants the same thing, or something quite similar, and you'll be on your way toward working on a mutual goal. Remember, though, there are no guarantees.

Another productive and enjoyable step is to tell your partner what you admire about his way of dealing with money matters. After all, everyone likes to be complimented. Focus on your partner's positive attributes. If you like how your partner pays the bills on time, organizes the tax records, and keeps the checkbook up-to-date, say so. If you're one of those tight-fisted types, you may envy the way your spouse is able to buy things without obsessing over the purchase. Maybe you'll even find some areas where you can grow and change by following your partner's example.

You'll probably not be surprised to hear that fights over money tend to get wild because of what one partner doesn't like about the other's financial approach. That's why your next important step is to be as diplomatic and as brief as possible when commenting on what bothers you about how your partner handles money. You don't want to defend or comment on each other's views. After you each *tactfully and concisely* state your case, you should take some time to think about what you've heard.

After You've Taken a Break, Pull Together the Paperwork Before You Start in Again

To strategize you'll need to know the financial facts of your life. Before you begin the next phase of your financial discussions with your partner, you should be able to point to some specifics about your spending patterns as a couple. Ideally, you should keep a daily log of expenses for a month or so, and categorize the spending before you go onto the second phase of your talk. You should keep track of expenses, including

- Rent or mortgage payments
- Utilities
- Food
- Restaurant meals
- Entertainment

- Credit card bills
- Car expenses
- Other transportation expenses
- Books, magazines, and newspapers

- Clothing
- Dry cleaning
- Insurance
- Miscellaneous minor expenses
- Babysitter and childcare expenses

- Sundries
- Beauty parlor
- Gifts
- Dues
- Charity
- Cable television

If you have occasional major expenses such as quarterly tax or insurance payments, be sure to prorate these items and include them in your breakdown.

In a nonthreatening way, go over the numbers with your partner. After these expenses, what is left over for discretionary spending and saving? If the situation is tight, ask what expenses your partner thinks could be cut back or eliminated. Be aware that the spender needs *some* latitude while the saver needs to be able to feel that *something* is being put away for a rainy day. Strive to find the middle ground. Look for alternatives that will work for each of you.

Both of you have needs, and neither person's needs are more important than the other's. By planning, both of you can have some of what you want. You must work to establish short, medium, and long-term goals. Make a chart and keep it handy to illustrate your mutual ongoing efforts toward meeting them.

When you encounter conflicts, try to guide the conversation back to each partner's broader needs, worries, and wishes, rather than the specifics of the dispute. If you end up focusing on what you don't agree on, the argument is likely to continue going around in circles. Look for even the smallest steps you can both take toward your mutual goals.

Avoid Vacation Fights Over Money: Plan Ahead

Although money styles may collide at any time, they may do so most noticeably during your vacation, when you're together 24 hours a day. If one of you wants to lie on a beach and the other is ready to undertake a major fishing expedition, you will need to work out a negotiated settlement. Ignoring the dispute will *not* work here and it may just turn your relaxation time into a major crisis.

To avoid having to take separate vacations or having constant arguments during joint ones, you must talk things over beforehand. If, for example, you're going camping, and one partner is acting as navigator while the other is in charge of pitching the tent, cleaning up, and performing all other chores, you might have an insurrection, not a vacation, on your hands. It's better to discuss who will be doing what well ahead of time.

Division-of-labor issues are one common type of vacation dispute. Other disagreements occur about how much to spend on accommodations, activities, food, and what to buy for yourself and friends.

When it rains during a Keeper's vacation, they may think of themselves as victims whose money has gone down the drain. They often don't feel they've gotten their money's worth unless they can swim, sunbathe, and make use of all the facilities available. The Power Seekers who get rained out can manage better, unless they happen to be golfers who cannot imagine any other form of recreation. Other Power Seekers may head to the designer boutiques or pricey restaurants for entertainment; the Love Buyers may pass the time there as well. The Freedom Searchers, however, probably won't mind the rain at all, and can be counted on to find some way to enjoy themselves, even during a tempest. Knowing these inclinations ahead of time may help you develop a workable "backup plan," one that even a Keeper could buy into ahead of time.

Let's assume a woman who is a Love Buyer is on a weekend getaway with a man who's a Freedom Searcher. Also assume that this couple didn't sit down together before the trip to work out a plan of what they each wanted to do. What situation is likeliest to lead to a major blowout between the two? Perhaps, she's in the mood for romance on the first night of the trip and she's got her heart set on a night of dinner and dancing in her fanciest gown. She wants her partner to let her know she is beautiful and loved. He also wants romance, but he's exhausted from his daily commuting grind and his idea of finding love is to spend some time together . . . alone. He wants room service and a spicy in-room movie, and no pressure. She won't even listen to his plan, mentioned at the last minute, since she's bought a new dress, shoes, and jewelry for the occasion. This unpleasant encounter could have been prevented if this couple planned ahead of time.

Don't leave home without first comparing fantasies! Take time beforehand to talk about how you want to spend your time and money.

How to Resolve Money Fights Once They Start

Resolving fights starts with using "I need" sentences. Here are some examples:

"I need a rest."

"I need a little love."

"I feel like I need a reward for the hard work I've done."

"I need to get our sex life back in order."

"I need to feel more comfortable about our level of control over our finances."

The next step? Try to initiate "How about if we . . ." compromises. Take whatever suggestion you feel will move you closer to the goal you've just outlined, and share it with your partner. Be sure you begin with some variation on "How about if we . . ."!

Listen to your partner's response. Repeat it back to him, and encourage him to talk about his needs and feelings, too, just as you have.

Be willing to compromise. Accept baby steps.

"Red Herring" Fights

Stan wants to take sailing lessons and is considering buying a boat if he finds that he really enjoys himself while he's learning. His wife, Kelly, likes sailing, but isn't crazy about the possibility of entertaining on a boat. She may complain by saying, "That seems like a lot of money to pay for sailing lessons." What she may really be concerned about is that Stan may eventually spend a lot of time away from her.

Most couples have "red herring" fights like these. In such conflicts, the partners are not really fighting over the key issue, but are masking their concerns by addressing other "problems." Unless the big issue is identified and discussed, it will continue to cause fight after fight—guaranteed.

If Kelly can clearly say that she needs some attention from Stan, Stan can explain how he feels so stressed out that he's desperate for some form of relaxation and needs some time to himself before being with her. Once these primary needs have been directly addressed, the two can plan how they can get away from the pressures of work and do things together that they both want to do. Neither is a mind reader. Each needs help from the other in learning what the most important issues are right now.

Talking about the real issues keeps the conflict from escalating to painful levels. If these partners don't talk about what's really bothering them, there's a real risk that Kelly may polarize the situation completely by yelling something like, "Sailing? With your sense of direction, you better stick to rides on the rowboats in Central Park!"

Listening Hurdles to Overcome

Many couples suffer from what I call "crooked hearing." They hear the words, but they get processed incorrectly. For example, John may say to Sue, "Nice dress—is it new?" Instead of answering the question directly, Sue assumes that what John is really saying is that he knows she went shopping for clothes despite his appeal to her last month that she not buy anything until the after-Christmas sales.

This scene may quickly become a fight, because Sue has "heard" John criticize her. She's made an assumption that John's mad. In fact, he isn't. He thought she bought a new dress, but actually, it was just one he hadn't seen for a long time. Sue read far too much into John's tone of voice, and even thought she saw a look in his eye that made her flinch. The result? She's on the defensive.

She could head off the fight by paying more attention to what John actually said instead of what she thought he said. On the other hand, she could also make matters more tense by preparing something to say in case John gets hot under the collar—which she fully expects. If she does, she'll be so busy thinking, "If he says this, I'll say . . ." that she could miss the next thing John actually says to her.

Sometimes, people filter out things they don't want to hear. Let's pretend for a moment that John really is mad about the new dress. Perhaps he concludes that Sue didn't hear him tell her that money was tight, and that the credit card was maxed out last month. He could get pretty huffy if he makes a faulty assumption that she filtered out this warning. Before he proceeds on this assumption, he should check that Sue is aware of the credit crunch. He might even win points for bringing this topic up at a later time, without fixating on the "new" dress. If, however, John silently blames Sue for their financial crunch, and thinks to himself, "She's such a spendaholic," he's likely to be too busy judging her to be able to listen to what she has to say. Once he starts calling her names in his mind, the only listening he's capable of is the kind that will justify his negative thoughts about Sue's spending habits. He cuts off any chance of having a constructive conversation simply because of the way he thinks about his partner.

As a general rule, women need to talk to feel better, and men need to give advice to feel helpful. Men who jump in with advice may have good intentions, but advice actually shuts off the flow of conversation. Women experience this "help" as a turn-off. Women who understand that men want to help can convey appreciation for a man's effort to "fix" things, but she will do well to make it clear that she wants time to be heard out. For example, Sue may want John to know that she'd like a new dress, but she really wanted a compliment for being able to fit into this one, which she hadn't been able to wear for a few seasons. To her, it feels like a new dress. The last thing she wants to hear now is a lecture about how she should limit her shopping to thrift shops!

Some couples never really have conversations. They have debates. They disagree, it seems, about everything. When one talks, the other automatically assumes the opposite position and defends it to the hilt. That's not a particularly effective way to go about solving a common problem.

Perhaps John likes to come across as being right all the time. Perhaps he has a tendency to fend off real or imagined criticism by means of his trademark appeals to logic and precedent. He'll have all the facts to justify his point of view and will coolly dismiss any arguments he feels are "too emotional." He doesn't listen to these arguments because he doesn't trust feelings. Sue, on the other hand, has emotions to spare, especially when she's reacting to John. She sometimes feels as though she's a boiling cauldron, one that bubbles over from time to time out of frustration with her inability to convince John of anything he doesn't want to listen to. This is a classic self-perpetuating cycle, one that keeps the partners from discussing important issues. The more emotional Sue is about her problems, the more likely John is to dismiss what she has to say as part of her "craziness." The more John takes this approach, the more furious Sue becomes.

If John could put his thoughts into feeling words, rather than lawyerly arguments, perhaps Sue would listen to him a little more. If Sue could be more precise in describing her feelings and what causes them, John might listen to her more.

If partners make a point of starting off each sentence with "I" instead of "You," they can learn to head off fights. When a woman tells her partner, "I feel like a kid without an allowance if I can't buy anything," her man can't realistically maintain that her feelings are wrong. She owns her feelings. There's no fight. It's only when she says to her partner, "Damn it! You make me so mad when you're cheap. If you don't change, then I'm not going to sock any more of my money into the new car fund," that her partner is moved to defend himself rather than to solve any problem.

Dealing Effectively with Conflicts

You'll stand a better chance of getting what you want without inflicting psychological damage on your partner or yourself if you:

1. Maintain receptive body language. Keep your arms unfolded, make nonthreatening eye contact, and don't point in an accusing way.

2. Try to describe how you feel without using a loud, cold, or sarcastic tone of voice. By concentrating on describing, you'll keep your blood pressure down. Attacking, on the other hand, raises it.

3. Convey your observations about the situation and explain what makes you so upset. To start, make a point of sticking to neutral, factual statements rather than opinions. Make sure that your statements do not amount to judgments about your partner. Edit out assumptions before you speak. After all, assumptions are often wrong.

4. Say what your thoughts are on the matter. Stay away from "facts." Explain how you interpret the situation. If you come across as

saying what your understanding of the situation is, you leave room for your partner to clarify or correct things. You can't be accused of "trying to be right all the time."

5. Specify what you need. You might say, "I need to get more attention from you," or "I need to feel that we're making progress in moving toward our goal of owning our own home."

6. Don't look for negatives in what your partner says or does.

7. Stay away from exaggerations. Remember that words like "disgusting," "ridiculous," and "always" have a way of fanning the flames.

8. Don't see issues as either white or black, right or wrong. Don't react as though your partner were the enemy. The fact that your needs have not been met—yet—does not make your mate a bad person. Be aware of the subtleties, the gray areas, that include feelings, needs, and motivations. These are things that complicate but enrich every interpersonal interaction.

9. Don't vent. Contrary to what you may think, yelling and engaging in emotional violence won't get you the cooperation or respect you want. Take a time-out if necessary.

10. Don't get defensive. When under attack, it's natural to try to protect yourself. Some methods of self-defense are not constructive, however. Avoidance, pretending there is no problem, and shutting down emotionally and/or sexually are examples of unproductive ways to behave when there are problems to be solved.

Chapter 9

Cheapskates, Spendthrifts, and Other Common Challenges

*M*ichael has always been frugal. After all, he comes from a large family and always had to work hard and save for whatever he wanted. Jeanne is the opposite: Her family is fairly comfortable and, although she doesn't consider herself extravagant, she has different tastes and habits than Michael. Some of Michael's habits—shopping at warehouse clubs and going to bargain movie matinees—are acceptable to Jeanne, but she's becoming increasingly frustrated at Michael's insistence that they find the absolute cheapest way to do everything. Their last vacation was nearly a disaster because they flew some new, no-frills airline that delayed their arrival by a day. The "budget" hotel accommodations were so bare that Jeanne thought she was staying in military barracks!

As you read earlier in this book, women are often socialized into conceding the lead role on financial matters to the men in their lives. This can lead to big problems, especially when the men in question are stuck in their own negative patterns. These patterns often have a profound effect on both people in the partnership. In this chapter, you'll learn how women can take a constructive approach to dealing with some of the most common problems and planning issues women may face as partners in a relationship.

What If You're in a Relationship with a Cheap Man?

The instincts of the Keeper, when pushed to the limit, may result in a lifestyle that is far too cheap for its own good. If this "Scrooge problem" seems to describe the man in your life, and if you've concluded that you don't share your cheapskate's outlook on life, you need to develop a strategy for constructive change.

Most of you have had some experience with these kinds of men. These are the men who invite you out for a drink . . . and do, in fact, mean for one single, solitary drink to be the extent of the evening's festivities. They make the decision to give your coat to the coat-check girl and, at evening's end, skip out of the restaurant ahead of you without tipping her, so you're left with the choice of tipping her yourself or walking away embarrassed. These men don't tip much for meals either, and the service doesn't have to be all that bad for them to stiff the waiter. After all, they may rationalize, why bother to tip mediocre service if they'll never see that server again? They don't like to split menu items, but they'll be glad to share the tab, provided, of course, that you ordered less than they did.

Not long ago, I appeared on a talk show where several hyper-cheap men confessed their eccentricities to the world. One would always turn his car's motor off and coast into his garage from the top of the hill, not because he was out of gas, but to save a few pennies. Another man boasted about reusing paper towels! There was a film clip of him rinsing out paper towels and hanging them on a little clothes line he'd rigged up over his sink. My favorite was the fellow who stopped in at a local bank every morning to take advantage of the free cup of coffee the financial institution offered to anyone who walked in the door. His girlfriend, who was about to leave him, said that she knew she had to think twice about the relationship when she saw her man take off his shoes and socks and climb into a fountain at the mall to collect the pennies people had thrown.

No matter how endearing these cheap guys may be, when they pinch pennies until their fingers hurt, they make it tough on people who don't share their outlook. Usually, there are no surprises. The cheap person with money will probably be cheap in his feelings, will take cheap vacations, give you cheap gifts, and go to cheap restaurants. Spending money on taxicabs or long-distance telephone calls is usually seen as a violation of a firmly held religious principle.

For most of you, hyper-cheap men are inherently unattractive. Most women are looking for men who are secure enough to treat them well and perform well in business and social situations. When that doesn't happen, resentment brews and percolates into anger—anger that, not infrequently, threatens the relationship's very existence.

These men, who usually stand a vigilant guard against the possibility that they may be taken advantage of, often "borrow" without returning, don't replace things they've used, and indulge in the unfortunate habit of taking what they need from others without asking first. Often, they'll spend an inordinate amount of time comparing prices on everything from toothpaste to tie clips but then turn around and complain that their day was too full to stop by the post office as they'd promised to do. They may deny themselves things that even the poorest people have, such as gloves during winter, as though they were repenting for some crime they committed in the nursery. It is not uncommon for these men to engage in one of these strange behaviors, all of them, or some new brand of cheapness to get of the title, World's Greatest Tightwad. These people—almost uniformly Keepers—are often trying to make up for not getting enough love or money during their childhood.

Guilt for real or perceived aggressiveness early in life is a factor in adult super-cheapness. Stinginess is a way of staying in control and still, in an odd way, being aggressive. After all, extreme frugality is certainly offputting and it does, as a practical matter, end many relationships, which may be the "punishment" these men think, deep down, that they deserve. Initially, these men can be charming, funny, and even endearing in their money habits. Eventually, though, they have a way of getting on your nerves.

If your man doesn't want to reform, and you want to stay in the relationship, you will need to help him look at his issues of guilt, insecurity, and control, and you will need to start helping him arrange his priorities. Otherwise, your man will continue to see money, rather than you, as his best friend. That's not the foundation of a healthy relationship.

Don't assume the worst! In evaluating your man's patterns, you shouldn't conclude that a few examples of stinginess are signs of a long-term problem.

Remember, there is a continuum of cheapness, so give your guy a chance to show you where he stands on that continuum. Just because he wants to take you to the local diner for dinner doesn't mean that he can't be more flexible in other ways. Pick your battles, and you may find that he's willing to give ground on areas of importance to you.

What if there seems to be little or no flexibility on any front? The more rigid the man, the more difficult and uncomfortable it will be for you to try to live with him. If your man really is at the far end of the Keeper/cheapskate scale, you may be buying into a partnership with a self-denying individual who has to prove that he can tolerate having less, and who will put himself at the bottom of every priority list. Guess what? That means you're at the bottom of the list, too.

The woman who finds this kind of a man attractive may be one who is perceived as spontaneous, fun-loving, and easygoing. She may see the man she picks as having his head set square on his shoulders and his feet planted firmly on the ground. In other words, she may assume that he possesses qualities that counteract her own potential negatives. She may be looking for a man who is practical and solid, and who forms a "good balance." This is all very well in theory, but the realities of the day-to-day relationship may prove quite challenging.

One way the scenario between these two types can play out results in a potentially disastrous cycle. His monthly obsessions about the bills take time and attention away from her, which leads to her making increasingly more extravagant and unbudgeted purchases as a reaction to the lack of interest and input. This leads to interest, all right, although it is entirely negative in nature. The pattern reinforces itself, as he gets more and more preoccupied with the bills and she feels more and more threatened and cut off. Both of them end up spending more and more time arguing about increasingly serious financial problems.

When dealing with a Keeper who has cheapskate tendencies, but who seems to have real potential as a partner, you don't want to engage in brinkmanship or attention-getting maneuvers—you want to stimulate positive change. This change can only occur if your man wants it to. You cannot move a mule by barking orders at it. Mules will sometimes move, though, if they think that the idea to move is theirs.

Before you turn away from your man, try to tap into his desire for more fun. You may find that he'll take advantage of the opportunities to lighten up, if he can enjoy himself. Start with special events like birthdays or anniversaries. After a number of suggestions of things you could do, things that actually cost money, and let him pick one. If he can shell out a few extra dollars on these occasions, and feel that he's gotten his money's worth as a result, he may be willing to change his behavior over time.

Let's assume that you and your partner keep separate bank accounts. You might suggest that the two of you share expenses and have a party for two or more friends. Having a good time together in this setting may make him feel like repeating the experience. You could start with cocktails and have your friends bring the nuts and chips. Maybe he'll cook along with you or make the salad—all the better if he shopped and paid for it! He'll like the compliments. The more he's "invested," the more he'll be involved.

Why not treat a cheap boyfriend to dinner once in a while? By doing so, you may be able to avoid an unpleasant conflict, and let your man see that there is real pleasure in paying for an evening without breaking the bank. Women may be expecting too much by assuming they'll be treated every time they go out. By happily paying the tab, you can show a cheap man how to enjoy himself—by example.

Another approach: The surprise getaway. Take the lead and tell your man, "I know a very special place I want to take you to." The air of mystery and excitement can help you break up old patterns and lay the foundation for new ones. Make the arrangements, and carry as much of the financial burden as you feel comfortable assuming. (Picking a modestly priced destination is probably a good idea.) The idea is not to lead your man to expect that you will always be there to whisk him away to some exotic locale. You don't want to build up a cycle of dependency, after all! What you're trying to demonstrate is that a little spontaneity and excitement can be a wonderful thing, and that relinquishing that tightfisted approach every once in a while can actually lead to pleasure.

What To Do If You're Unmarried but Sharing Living Arrangements with a Cheap Man . . .

Ask yourself this important question—Are you feeling resentful a good deal of the time? If the answer is "yes," that may be a signal that you are being taken advantage of.

Live-in arrangements have a way of clarifying things. Does your man consider his presence to be "present" enough to compensate for everything else on your list? Think for a moment and consider the patterns that have been established thus far. If your live-in lover:

> regularly uses your shampoo, dental floss, and whatever else he needs without replacing anything or even addressing the subject,

> never chips in for groceries,

> spends more than half of his time at your place, but doesn't pay rent,

> never takes out the garbage or performs other household chores,

then you have a right to feel exploited. You also have a right to ask straight out for changes in the relationship. Tell your man exactly how you feel about the current state of your relationship. (Some ideas on doing this appear a little later in this chapter. The next chapter outlines some ways to deal with this problem before you commit to a live-in relationship.)

Don't be surprised to hear your man respond that he, too, will feel resentful if you make him spend money that he doesn't feel he can afford. Super-cheapskates, however, don't feel that they can afford any money. How can you tell if you're dealing with someone who has an outlook problem, rather than someone who is facing a legitimate financial hurdle? The man in the former category will show a certain coldness in his voice and a tightness in his features, and will show not the faintest trace of remorse at the situation you describe. A man who really can't afford to help contribute to household expenses or go out with you will, more often than not, sound more regretful and sad about what you've described.

If you find you're constantly running up against a brick wall, and that your man shows no personal disappointment at any time about the problems you have with the current financial setup, you should think long and hard before you let your live-in arrangement become a permanent part of your life.

Here are some tips for talking about how your man's cheapness affects you, and about the changes you'd like to see in your relationship.

- When it comes time to talk, be aware of your feelings and express them. Tell your man that you feel angry, irritated, frustrated, or whatever. You don't have to get worked up, and you don't have to cry.

- Let him know that you've noticed how much he likes to stay with you, but that it surprises you that he hasn't done much to make living together more of a partnership. Give him a few examples of some of the things he could do to make you feel less discontented. For instance, ask if he could call you before coming home from work and ask whether he should pick something up from the supermarket, or if he'd ask what he could do around the house, or voluntarily clean off the table or make the bed.

- Come up with a suggested amount of money you would like for rent, but think twice before you suggest splitting this expense down the middle. This relationship may be ready for share-and-share alike status . . . and then again, it may not. If you're not crazy about the idea of beer-buddy get-togethers for the Big Game, or if you want to have the option of ordering your man off the premises if things don't work out, you'll be in a better position if you're paying most of the rent. But you certainly shouldn't have to pay all of it.

- Ask that your man keep track of his expenses for a month so he can see where his own money is going. Offer to track your expenses, too. Put stars next to those expenses where he participates, but doesn't pay, such as newspaper and magazine subscriptions, telephone, and cable. After the month has passed, ask him to contribute. If you're buying food, doing his laundry, or steaming his suits, put a price on these services and tell him that he can no longer expect to have all of this for free.

If things don't seem to be moving in the direction you want them to, let your man know that he's on probation for three months. Tell him that you need to see some action and change in that period, or you will have to end the relationship. Then follow through as promised if nothing happens. Do not make this threat if you don't intend to carry it out!

Coping with Spendthrift Men

Lori met Arthur in a writing class. He was the editor of a trade publication; he hoped to write the Great American Novel. One evening, they had coffee after class, and he asked if she'd go out with him that Saturday night. She said yes.

Arthur took her to one of the swankiest spots in New York, the Four Seasons Hotel, where they had drinks. Then he took her to a three-course-dinner at the best seafood place in town. At the end of the evening, the two enjoyed a horse-drawn carriage ride through Central Park under a full moon. Arthur paid for everything.

"I adored being taken out like this," said Lori. "He acted as if price was no object, but I was tallying up the tabs with tips and taxi cabs, and I couldn't help but wonder how he could afford this kind of night out on his salary. He continued to spend lavishly every weekend, charging everything, and treating me like a princess. I learned later on that he was deeply in debt on his numerous credit cards, and then I realized that this guy had a big problem. I had to tell him that while I appreciated how he treated me, it frightened me to be involved with someone who was so unrealistic about money."

It's nice to be encouraged to order the Blue Point oyster appetizer, the lobster, and the taramitsu for dessert. It's flattering to enjoy the finest wines and the most exotic coffee. But it can also be a danger signal, a tip-off that you are dealing with a Love Buyer who has a serious problem dealing with money. Extravagance may be the way to work out some deep-seated emotional issues.

Heavy-duty spending can mask heavy-duty insecurities. Many men—often those threatened by female earning power—need to bolster their sense of self-esteem by spending lavishly on rugged and/or high-tech "toys" such as full-scale camping gear or elaborate, state-of-the-art stereo systems. That they cannot afford these toys does not enter into the picture. Buying these items represents a way of saying, "I'm in charge here." Such men work hard to prevent fears of failure, vulnerability, and humiliation from surfacing; even those with low incomes will spend extravagantly to offset those nagging worries.

Roy was a consultant who earned $90,000 a year. He seemed to spend it all on restaurants. Eating out was his only pleasure. Indeed, it was more important than setting aside money to plan for his retirement, keep up on his other bills, or pay his taxes. The IRS eventually reminded him, as it has a way of doing, that such behavior does not go unnoticed.

A desire for love was motivating his eating spree. In his favorite places, he was treated royally since he frequently brought his friends along and because he was a generous tipper, the maitre d', wine steward, and coat-check girl all paid special attention to him. He used his restaurant visits to buy himself some special attention and pampering. He needed love, and since he was unsure of his own ability to love and be loved, he got temporary appreciation by taking dates and friends out to dinner and feeling adored for his generosity. He made up, or at least tried to compensate, for the lack of a love life at home by getting top-level treatment at a number of expensive restaurants.

What if you were involved with Roy? Chances are that you'd find yourself feeling the same way that people involved with gamblers, alcoholics, and drug addicts feel.

Roy is a compulsive spender, a spendaholic. He uses, or really abuses, money to get what he needs emotionally, and he *has to* do it a lot. His spending is totally out of control. He isn't able to cope with his uncomfortable feelings such as anxiety, so he makes them vanish—albeit temporarily—with the fix he gets by eating out. Then, as with compulsive shoppers, eaters, and drinkers, compulsive spenders, like Roy, must deal with the crash that follows. A period of deep shame, guilt, confusion, and depression usually sets in. When that black cloud lifts, the unbearable anxiety returns, and the cycle begins again. In Roy's case, it usually began again at dinnertime.

It isn't always easy to know whether you're dealing with a compulsive spender or a very generous person on the upper end of the income scale, but you don't have to be a private investigator to be able to make an educated guess about whether he can actually afford his expenses. If he pays by credit card, does he use one or is he shuffling three or four of them? Does he seem upset with his spending habits? Are you upset by them? Do you notice that he buys things that he never uses? If you ever see him tackle a pile of bills, ask yourself how he goes about paying them. Does he proceed in an orderly way through the pile, or does he play "eenie-meenie-mynie-moe?"

If your observations point to two or three of these danger signs, your man probably needs help. Therapy, self-help groups, Debtors Anonymous, and credit counseling services can help, provided he's willing to discuss the possibility of taking advantage of them. Getting to that point may take a while.

You know that what this big spender is really after is some demonstration of love, so your first step should be to try giving him lots. Hugs and kisses are free. Reassure him that intimacy and closeness are things he doesn't have to pay for. Talk to him about your concerns, and ask about his; make it clear that you care for him as a person, independent of financial concerns. Learn about the goals that are important to him, and don't dismiss them as fantasies, but do address them realistically. If, like Arthur, your man is hoping to get a big advance on an unwritten book, let him know that you'd prefer to spend what you have rather than what he might eventually earn. If your man will talk about his money behavior, he'll be in a better position to know that he needs to get help, so hold off on telling him to "see somebody about this problem" and instead, build a case with your observations and reactions.

Once you have found a pattern, you can try to bring his attention to all the clues he's left for you. Make your case by appealing to specific examples. Tell your man that there's a serious issue here, one that has to be addressed. Remember that you're always on firm ground when you talk about how his behavior affects you.

Prenuptial Agreements

How is one partner's insistence on a prenuptial agreement likely to affect a relationship? Will it throw a negative shadow over the future, one that needn't have been cast? Will it strengthen the bond between the two partners? Will it end the relationship?

"These agreements used to be only for the wealthy," Christina remarked during lunch with friends, "but today you have to be realistic since marriages don't always succeed. We all know the divorce rate is high. It's important to protect your assets."

Sandy disagreed. "I have a problem with the whole concept of a prenuptial agreement," she said. "Engagement time is supposed to be a time to commit to each other for the long haul . . . but then you sit down to discuss what you're going to do if it all comes apart. It's like dooming the marriage before it begins. Maybe you won't like what he asks you to agree to. What happens next? Cry and storm out? It feels like you're starting off in a negative way."

"But if you feel that threatened at the start," Pat asked, "why are you getting married?"

It's natural for people to have conflicting reactions to the prospect of a prenuptial agreement. A woman who brings substantial assets to the marriage is likely to have a very different view of the matter than a woman of lesser means. If a man asks you to sign a prenuptial agreement, you may find yourself wondering, "If you really love me, why are you asking me to go through this? It makes me feel like you don't trust me. Do you think I'm going to turn into a demon and steal from you?"

While you may think of men as the ones who are most likely to want a prenuptial agreement, the emergence of the two-income family means it is very often in a woman's best interest to have one also. A sound agreement, concluded in writing and made before any trouble arises, can help her through the difficult transition of a divorce, should one occur. Things like health insurance, moving expenses, and job retraining funds can and should be asked for. This issue has less to do with trust than it does with looking ahead, planning while you're in love as opposed to when you're not, and engaging in some thoughtful problem-solving. More and more middle-class partners are considering pre-nuptial agreements because of the high risk of divorce. Women need to know that they will be adequately taken care of, especially if there are children involved.

That's not sexism; that's reality. Research shows that if a woman leaves the workplace to have children and care for a home and spouse, she will, by age 50, have lost 3 percent of her earning potential for each year she was out of the work arena. That's a considerable amount of money to give up to be a mother and homemaker. She also loses Social Security coverage on those earnings. She needs reassurance and support, and an intelligent prenuptial agreement is a good way to attain these goals.

Do you take the romance out of the marriage by asking your mate-to-be to sign an agreement? Well, you certainly can, but you don't have to. It's all in the timing. The problem is that discussions of prenuptial agreements tend to come up at precisely the wrong time—shortly before the wedding! There probably isn't any "good" time to deal with these sensitive issues, but it's best to have your discussions long before the wedding day. The engagement period is a time of crisis and stress. Try not to wait until then to talk about how you learned about money, how your family handled it, and how your styles differ. After all, money is a reality to be dealt with on a daily basis—it is a fact of life. Address the issue early on.

Working on a prenuptial agreement may make it seem like you're headed for divorce instead of marriage, but making full financial disclosure to one another can actually help you to start the marriage off in an open manner. Negotiating the agreement forces the two of you to talk directly about money and helps you break the ice so that once you're married, finances won't be a taboo subject. Starting out by being honest with one another sets a good precedent for the long term.

If you or your partner refuses to sign and you come to an impasse, it's time to seek out a therapist who can help you communicate about money and uncover any hidden agendas that may need to be explored. If you can't talk about money matters before you get married, maybe you won't be able to later on either.

Not everyone has to have a prenuptial agreement, but it's an option you may want to consider when your circumstances warrant it. If you opt not to make an agreement part of your partnership, be sure that your decision does not deny or minimize money issues with your partner. Your differences in handling money will surface later on in your marriage, whether you want them to or not. It is best to address them as they surface.

What About Wills?

Many of today's parents are in that "sandwich generation" caught between aging parents and the needs of their own growing children. Just as they might have trouble talking with their parents about estate planning, they have trouble talking with each other. Many young parents put off drawing up a will because they are uncomfortable dealing with the topic of death, and are uneasy about confronting their own feelings toward their money.

If you are a parent who falls into this category, there are important reasons to overcome these and similar obstacles. Since there are decisions to be made about who would take care of your children in the event of your death, the ambivalence you might feel toward your closest relatives or friends can keep you from naming them as guardians, but you owe it to your family to discuss the issue with the appropriate people and make a choice.

After making mental notes about all of your friends' and relatives' parenting styles, you should have a talk with the "winners" and see if those you chose are willing to take on the responsibility of raising a child. You should offer a thumbnail sketch of the financial and insurance arrangements such a guardian would have to make sense of. Above all, you should take action now and not leave the decision to someone else.

Consider the various elements of the worst case scenario. After you die, custody of your kids could be assigned to the person in your family least able to deal with the job of raising a family, or to a complete stranger. Your children could be separated and sent to homes in different states. Your finances might be handled by someone who disagrees with the children's guardian on important matters.

The emotional factors of drawing up a will are difficult, but once you and your spouse agree to face the task, you will find that the picture falls into place quite easily. A simple will is inexpensive and quite basic.

If you've been meaning to get around to drawing up a will, but haven't found a way to make the time, consider the positive feelings you'll have when you know that you've pulled this part of your planning together. You will be able to enjoy the feeling that comes along with knowing you've acted as responsible adults. There's a secure feeling that comes with the certainty that you're prepared for an emergency. Pretending that emergencies don't occur, by contrast, is likely to make you feel much more anxious than you should, because you know it's not so! By taking care of your children in this way, you are loving parents. In addition, you'll rest secure knowing that you've gotten the details down on paper and eliminated a lot of potential problems. You will be the one to decide where your children and assets will go, and that's as it should be.

Chapter 10

Fifty/Fifty . . . and Fights?

Amy and Stuart

*A*my said it would be fine for Stuart to stay with her while he settled into his new job in the city. His commuter train rides to and from the suburbs had been a hassle, especially since he often had to stay late to entertain clients over dinner at restaurants. It was easier to stay at Amy's.

Stuart didn't offer to pay any rent; Amy didn't ask for any. The arrangement simply unfolded, without much planning beforehand on either of their parts. She did Stuart's laundry, sewed up the holes in his socks, handled most of the cooking, and generally supported him as he went about his business. Every once in a while, he would take her out to movies and inexpensive dinners on the weekends. Once in a while he passed along a modest gift. But he never made any financial contribution to the household.

Over time, Amy began to feel that this arrangement wasn't an equitable one. She liked Stuart's company and enjoyed having him as a lover, but all too often his stinginess reminded her of her own father's frugality, which was legendary in her family. Furthermore, Stuart, like Amy's father, didn't do anything to help out. He never shopped, never took out the garbage, and never offered to buy coffee or any of the other items he used regularly. Amy started to feel used and resentful.

When she told Stuart this, he became very tense and explained that he didn't want to move in on a permanent basis, that he had his own expenses at his own home to consider, and that he'd feel resentful of her if she asked him for rent or, for that matter, for more nights on the town or weekends away.

If Amy and Stuart had developed some kind of a mutually workable financial plan from the start, they might have been able to avoid this impasse, and the relationship probably could have flourished. As it was, things went downhill after Amy raised her feelings about financial issues. The topic would come up again and again, with the same result. Stuart insisted on maintaining the status quo. Amy resented the status quo. Stuart could tell that she resented it, and communication became strained. It got to the point where he even refused to give her a backrub. Eventually, Amy couldn't stand it any more. Just because her mother put up with her father didn't mean she had to live with someone just like him. She asked Stuart to leave.

Whether you're living with a man without the benefit of a marriage license, or helping to make decisions as a partner in a marriage, you will frequently be dealing with shared expenses. It is important to develop strategies for dealing with money questions within the context of an ongoing relationship, whether or not that relationship has legal status.

Living Together?

Joseph and Geri

When Joseph moved in with his girlfriend Geri, he agreed to pay half of all the rent and household expenses. Once he did, some changes took place in the relationship. Geri first noticed the changes when she realized that her live-in lover now felt he was entitled to complete control of the remote control for the television. They watched what he wanted to, period. Geri felt funny about making a big deal out of something so trivial as a television program or two, so she let him have his way. But there were more changes on the way. Joseph also felt that he was well within his rights to invite his teenage daughters to stay for weekends. His other relatives also found occasional free lodging in what used to be Geri's apartment, usually with little or no advance notice.

Joseph started to leave his clothes around the apartment until he was good and ready to pick them up—which usually meant that Geri picked them up, because she couldn't stand waiting until he got around to doing it. Joseph liked to cook, and to cook fairly extravagant dishes, at that. So Geri suddenly found herself paying more money for food in a single week than she used to spend all month.

Geri went along with all the new ways of doing things for a while, but after about a month she erupted. She missed the freedom she had come to associate with living in her own home, and she missed having at least some of the control that Joseph had suddenly appropriated. Geri found it quite hard to win an equal say in decisions with Joseph, and she couldn't see trying to build a life with him on the terms he seemed to demand. She asked him to leave. She admitted afterwards that she couldn't get used to having "someone else's habits shoved down my throat."

Too much partnership? Too little partnership? As more people choose to live together, whether as a preliminary to marriage, as an alternative to wedded life, or in order to enjoy a good time for a relatively short period, there are many financial angles to consider. The way you address them will have a great deal to do with how happy you are in the relationship, as the two stories above illustrate.

Discussing things ahead of time, and in detail, is the best way to deal with the problems you may face in a live-in relationship. Here are some of the questions you and your partner should address, preferably before you move in together on a formal or informal basis.

- Who pays the rent and utility bills? What would equal payment in these areas entitle each member of the relationship to when it comes to day-to-day domestic responsibilities, personal routines, and upkeep of the house or apartment?

- Who buys food and who pays for weekend entertainment? What does each person expect from the other as a result of contributions in these categories?

- If you both enjoy newspapers and magazines, who pays for the subscriptions?

- If you both contribute to buy items meant to furnish or decorate your joint home, who owns the new things if you split up?

- In a two-income household, who will actually take time to purchase the items you need? (Many men are uneasy about assuming a role here, even when their partners provide 50 percent or more of the household's income. If you don't want to deal with all the shopping chores, you should talk about this early on.)

Sounds complicated, doesn't it? Well, it is. Since there's no marriage contract, it's possible, theoretically at least, for either partner to say "the heck with this relationship," and walk out without any obligations. You may think that's not such a big deal if you're talking about a month's worth of financial issues, but short-term arrangements have a way of turning into long-term arrangements. It's best to address all of these complexities early on in the process.

Even in casual relationships, you should sit down together and talk about your expectations. How do you plan to handle things financially? The answers may point you toward deeper issues in your relationship that are worth reviewing. One woman may harbor a fantasy of being taken care of by her chosen man, as her mother may have been, while her man may desire to be nurtured, perhaps as his father was. Even casual live-ins will have to make compromises on such issues. One of you will likely emerge as more of a decision-maker than the other.

Even in the short term, partners bring their own predispositions to the table, and must develop strategies for dealing with important questions. The issue is whether or not those strategies will be implemented consciously, or will be allowed to develop haphazardly, in ways that are likely to breed discontent. The idea is to address problems in depth, not issue simple pronouncements or principles. The person who dismisses details with the vow that he or she "wants a 50/50 relationship when it comes to finances" may find making this a daily reality a very difficult task. On some issues, one person is likely to want to take the lead; on others, it may be necessary to switch roles.

Here are some guidelines that can help you establish some workable "house rules" in the absence of the legal commitment of marriage:

■ Keep your money separate. Each of you should have your own credit cards and bank accounts. The last thing you need is to have your credit ruined—or your savings account wiped out—by an angry lover with signing privileges.

■ Keep a written record of what you buy yourself. Should you or your lover decide to leave, it will be helpful if you have a running list of things you paid for independently. However, if you paid for the cocktail table because your live-in agreed to pay for something else, you both own the table, and you'll have to compromise as you divide the spoils.

■ Establish a household petty cash envelope for such things as cleaning supplies, shampoo, and light bulbs. Each partner should insert a couple of twenty-dollar bills into the envelope at the beginning of the month. If you occasionally order out for food, this is a good cash source for dealing with those types of expenses, too.

■ Decide who pays for what, how, and when. If there is an income disparity, you may want to divide the expenses proportionately while making it clear that this doesn't give one partner more decision-making power than the other. (Remember the battle of the television remote! Consider heading off power-plays earlier, rather than later.) Beware of dividing things 50/50 if one person earns less than the other does. There's no guarantee that this plan will give you equality in decision-making, and the person without any discretionary money is likely to feel some resentment by the time the end of the month rolls around.

■ It's very likely that one of you is more adept at wading through piles of bills than the other. Let that person write out the monthly checks; the other person should write a single reimbursement check to the bill-paying partner before the month is out.

■ Remember that living together is, statistically speaking, almost certainly a temporary state of affairs. If you don't commit to each other and get married, the odds are that you'll break up within a few years. It's a good idea to maintain your independence and resist falling into traditional sex roles during this phase. Try for "partnership" status instead of consenting to a relationship in which you have no economic power.

■ If yours is a special situation and you're older, divorced, or widowed, or have some other reason for making a strategic decision to live together on a long-term basis, you may want to talk to a lawyer about how to handle things if you and your partner decide to own property together. There may be some complex issues to consider, including whether your children from prior marriages will inherit your assets. (See also the points in Chapter 14 on the financial issues associated with aging parents.)

■ If you're each independent, and will each be paying for your individual expenses most of the time, decide what to do about infrequent "favors" with monetary implications. What happens if one partner picks up the laundry? If you are a Keeper, will you expect strict reimbursement for every expenditure? If your partner is a Power Seeker, will he simply stop doing any and all favors that have even the vaguest connection to money, even if this leads to serious inconvenience? You may have to develop compromises to deal with such situations, but it's better to do so now than to risk disappointment and misunderstanding later on.

Married?

For sure, living together doesn't carry the same sense of commitment, trust, or feeling of ongoing unity that marriage does. Pooling money is more common in marriage than reimbursing one's partner; joint ownership of property, and bank and credit accounts, is the way couples usually, but not always, choose to set things up. Nevertheless, your past experiences—whether they are rooted in the experience of being single, your early influences, or the ordeal of having been burned financially as an adult—can lead to some tricky situations.

Making the transition from single status to marital bliss isn't easy. Your way of doing things probably differs from your partner's. If you've taken pride in paying your own way, or grown used to dividing the check 50/50 no matter who had the dessert, you'll bring your financial slant to the bargaining table when it's time to decide who pays for what in your own household.

The way a couple handles money questions is one barometer of the state of the relationship as a whole. Consider Karen and Bill, who divide all expenses according to their ability to pay. Since Bill makes 25 percent more than Karen does, he contributes that extra amount to the kitty for such things as rent, vacations, utilities, entertainment, and food. "We decided when we married to maintain the sense of freedom we had when we took care of ourselves. It took a lot of hard work to become independent, and we treasure it too much to give it up," Karen says firmly. When they got married, they made a chart of all the household expenses and saw in black and white what had to be paid out on a weekly, monthly, or quarterly basis. The money left was for each of them to use as they wished for personal expenses, gifts, and savings. He pays for his and she pays for hers.

Karen's declaration of independence reflects her belief that paying her own way is the only fair way to carry her part of the load. She and Bill appear to be equal partners in making decisions through this "prorated" system. There are some disadvantages, they agree: They spend a lot of time on bookkeeping, they are always on the lookout for rate and price changes, and they find that big-ticket items threaten to reduce their discretionary money too much. As a result, Karen and Bill have had to make some compromises when it comes to the quality of their furnishings. At times, they concede, it feels like they are still living together, rather than committed for the long haul. What Karen and Bill may come to realize is that their wish for autonomy may be at the price of mutuality. With more sharing and less fear of losing their separateness, they may grow into their roles as equal partners.

Other couples "handle" their household money in a way that is distinctly one-sided. He earns the money, hands it over to her, and she hands out an allowance to him. For some people, it makes sense to have one partner take charge of all the bills and major financial decisions. For some of you, however, reporting to a financial "boss" means getting bossed around, and that may lead to some important emotional issues for both sides to review.

In a good many marriages, the person who holds the purse strings may exercise the power to give or withhold money a little too energetically for the other partner's tastes. Some partners lose self-esteem by having to ask for money constantly, or having to account for it after every expenditure. If children get allowances, and can manage their own money without strings attached, adults deserve the same level of trust and respect.

In the end, this issue boils down to attitude, rather than the specific, formal arrangements you or your partner may implement. When one adult makes it clear that he or she is "allowing" another to spend money, the relationship has more in common with a parent/child bond than that of two mature adults.

Wendy and Jeffrey

Wendy and Jeffrey had discussed in detail the pitfalls that each of their parents experienced in addressing financial matters. The couple vowed not to have the fights over money in their marriage that they overheard at home as children. They started out with one checking account, but Jeffrey quickly reacted negatively to having to pay for "facials, regular fingernail appointments, and accessories in rainbow colors every month." He knew his salary as a lawyer easily covered these items, but he wasn't prepared to underwrite what he saw as his wife's frivolous expenses. "How many belts does a woman need?" he asked.

Wendy felt that she had a right to buy the things she could afford, but she also understood that "rubbing Jeffrey's nose in the bills" was unnecessary. The couple decided to set up separate sub-accounts, each targeted exclusively for "personal pleasures." The move led to peace on the home front.

In situations such as Wendy and Jeffrey's, there may be a good case to be made for pooling funds in a single checking account for household expenses, and setting up separate, smaller accounts for each partner to use for personal purchases. Such an arrangement may allow you to avoid conflicts that only serve to infuriate one or both partners. After all, many men tire quickly of the old battle-cry: "What's mine is mine, and what's his is ours." By setting up a system that allows for a big "ours," and two smaller, limited "mines," you may be able to sidestep much needless bickering.

Once you recognize each other's spending and investing styles, and set up separate accounts that help you avoid fights about the small stuff, establishing the priorities for your shared long-term goals will almost certainly be easier than it was before. A little accommodation toward your partner's point of view can go a very long way indeed.

Some households operate inefficiently because financial tasks are carried out by the wrong person. The symptoms are bounced checks, stacks of paperwork lying around in no particular order, and constant fights over money, fights that may really be about the division of labor, regardless of the content of the discussion. As with a living-together arrangement, you will need to take the time to determine who is best suited to handle routine financial chores. Remember, computers and software make financial management much easier than it once was. If one of you is more of a computer aficionado than the other, you may be able to solve the division-of-labor problem by running the finances with the help of a PC, something one partner enjoys doing.

What are the best rules to follow when it comes to assigning financial tasks? There are two.

1. Even a partner who's busy all the time can make life easier by agreeing to drop bills into the mailbox or make bank deposits once in a while.

2. If you enjoy doing a job, it should probably be yours. Some people find filing, organizing, and reconciling to be supremely relaxing pursuits. If you fall into this category, you may be the best person for the checkbook-balancing job. Give it a try!

You should set aside time for discussing money matters on a regular basis. Going over fixed and flexible expenses together can be a real eye-opener. Face the questions and challenges together. When emotions get in the way, you'll probably find it's because old ideas and ungratified needs have surfaced. If you want to feel depended on, or dependent on someone else, it's better to talk the matter through than to try to use money to talk for you.

Finding what works best for you may take some trial and error. Don't censure yourself for making mistakes. Seeing what has to be done and volunteering for the jobs available may help you head off power struggles; questioning the division of labor if things don't seem to be operating well may help you correct imbalances. Communicating your feelings about wanting to know and wanting to be involved in the financial facts of life will help to maximize peaceful coexistence within your relationship. Since rewards are the key incentive to changing behavior patterns, don't forget to give yourself, and each other, those well-deserved pats on the back. Rewards aren't just a good idea—they're indispensable.

Here are some steps you can take that will help encourage a harmonious approach when it comes to dealing with the shared financial tasks in your marriage.

- Keep all the bills, stamps, envelopes, and checks in a convenient place.

- Pay the bills regularly, once or twice a month.

- Keep your checkbook up to date. If you have a joint account and each of you has an ATM card, keep all the receipts in a special envelope.

- File old bills and receipts.

- Don't let bills and unopened mail pile up.

- Talk once a month or so about your financial goals; discuss your progress toward them. Monitor the quality of your bookkeeping. Share ideas on how the two of you might improve things.

- Reward yourselves appropriately for keeping on top of your personal finances.

Part IV

Money and Other Significant Others

Chapter 11

Family Matters

lise had a challenging job as an investment banker before having her first child. She had always intended to return to work, but she found that she enjoyed staying home with her son. When her six months of leave were up, she resigned. Now, she's pregnant again and can't foresee returning to work in the near future. While Elise is happy with her choice, she finds that she frequently has to justify her decision to others.

You may hear homemakers—those women who decide not to pursue professional careers—referred to as "women who don't work," but this is laughable. These women work hard—and constantly—but because they're not getting a paycheck, they tend to drop off the world's economic map.

Homemakers often work much longer hours than most paid workers, and they sometimes have to beg and plead for even meager amounts of spending money. Their perks are determined by their husbands' jobs, as are health and pension benefits. In the event of divorce, a homemaker can usually expect to continue the health insurance from her husband's job for only a set number of months at her own expense. If a marriage lasts less than ten years, a woman may find that she's not eligible for any of her husband's pension. And many divorced women must suddenly face the many perplexing problems of single life, including how to suddenly establish a career or renew one that thay left years before. What does a newly single woman with significant childcare responsibilities, and whose resume features a 10- or 12-year "blank spot," as the business world is likely to

perceive it, do to start or reinvigorate her career? The answers to this difficult question probably lie beyond the scope of this book. The fact remains,
though, that the level and degree of financial rewards women receive for
their work within the family is, in most cases, simply not in accordance
with their contributions.

> Raising children, as important as you know it is, is still seen as low-status or
> no-status work. This fact can give rise to some significant self-esteem prob-
> lems, especially for women who are used to bringing home a paycheck in a
> past "incarnation."

All the same, the work you choose to undertake within the family is
valid, important, and enriching work, whether or not the rest of the world
recognizes it as such. It may take even more effort to retain your healthy
self-image in the face of these social and economic pressures and disadvantages, but that effort is essential.

In this chapter, you'll examine some of the key financial issues you
and your partner are likely to face in your roles as parents. Also, you'll
explore some of the challenges that arise from the fact that today's society,
as a general rule, doesn't value jobs that don't pay. You'll also learn the best
ways to communicate with your children about money matters—an
important topic for moms and dads alike.

Pregnancy and Parenthood

If you and your spouse have not yet had your first child, but are considering doing so, there are some topics you will probably want to review
together to help prepare for the difficult but rewarding job of starting a
family. Here are some issues to explore as you ponder the important stage
of life you are about to enter.

- If you plan to stop working, what will life be like with one paycheck? How will each of you deal with the task of establishing new
  spending priorities with only one check coming in?

- Do you agree on how long you will stay at home with your child?

■ Do you agree on how you are going to go about handling the new expenses a baby brings?

If you leave the workplace to stay at home with your baby, you may find that you miss the camaraderie of colleagues, the structure of the work day, and the intellectual challenge of new projects. You may feel socially isolated, physically tired from constant baby care, and mentally unstimulated.

If you don't return to work after a moderate pregnancy leave, you'll also have to face the issue of whether to enter or re-enter the job market after your child reaches an age at which he or she could spend some time with a babysitter in daycare. If you're addressing this situation, you'll have to confront a bewildering array of questions including:

How much will child care cost?

How do these childcare expenses impact the "additional" income you will be bringing to the household?

What about meals, transportation, and clothing?

What about the emotional "cost" associated with not "being there" full time for your child or children?

A man will also have his own money adjustments to make as part of the process of becoming a parent, especially if he is the only source of financial support for the family. Remember that being the sole breadwinner can be a very daunting task indeed. Certainly, any working single parent can attest to this fact!

Many men feel trapped in their jobs after the arrival of a new baby. They may feel they cannot afford to try new things or take time out for themselves anymore. If the man feels he must now maintain as much as he can of what used to be a two-paycheck lifestyle, and if he has only a single paycheck with which to perform this task, he may feel a strong sense of personal sacrifice . . . or even deep and long-lasting resentment. He may note with some bitterness that, even though he's working as hard as, or harder than, he ever did, there's less money for dinners out, vacations, and entertainment. A new mother may feel a certain disappointment at these developments, too, but a man who has staked a large chunk of his own personal identity on maintaining his status level—as defined by income—may feel a special kind of letdown, and a disturbing feeling of suffocation, as he surveys the post-baby economic landscape.

This sense of deprivation may be the motivating factor among some men who make expensive credit purchases shortly after the birth of a child, seemingly without any reason. These men may feel a profound dissatisfaction, so buying new things is their way of dealing with this problem. A major purchase can temporarily salve a sagging ego. If you spot signs of such trouble, take the opportunity to discuss the underlying issues with your mate right away. Dealing with real or imagined feelings of neglect or low self-esteem openly and as early as possible may help you avoid a dangerous financial spiral.

It's a good idea to use the intelligent communication methods outlined earlier in this book to nip such crises early, because kids in general, and new babies in particular, tend to cost a lot of money. When you figure in doctors' bills, diapers, cribs, carriages, layettes, and lost income—not to mention future expenses such as braces, educational savings, and the occasional prom dress—you realize there will be plenty of new expenses to deal with on a regular basis. Usually, you'll have less money than you'd like for all of these expenses.

Discuss your and your partner's underlying money issues. Head off any looming spending-pattern problems along the lines just outlined, or as explained earlier in this book. Do this now, rather than later. Growing families can't afford lots of financial setbacks.

Of course, nobody can really "afford" a financial crisis. The fact that there will soon be children in your family, however, establishes the need for a financially stable home environment—one in which emotionally charged exchanges are kept to a workable minimum, and positive financial lessons are learned easily.

What Do Kids Need to Know About Money?

Babies, of course, have a way of turning into children and, as you read in Chapter 2, early childhood experiences can have a great deal to do with the development of money attitudes. Therefore, it's very important that you try to teach your kids to develop healthy attitudes about money. The best way to do this, of course, is by using your own example as the primary teaching tool.

The single most important lesson about financial matters that you should teach your kids—through both your words and your deeds, is pretty straightforward:

Money is not the answer to the basic human psychological needs. If it were, those with the most cash would be the happiest people on earth. They're not.

Basic, human-to-human needs, the ones that motivate us most strongly, are the same for children as they are for adults. They do not require lots of money to fulfill. Parents have the responsibility to teach their children that security, love, independence, and power can be achieved independently. Learning to reinforce oneself is, after all, an essential part of the maturing process that you, as a parent, are supposed to foster. But becoming self-reliant is also, paradoxically enough, the work of a lifetime for most people.

You and your child can learn this important dual lesson about self-reliance—and its relation to financial issues—together if need be. If this is the way your relationship with your child seems to be unfolding, don't criticize yourself. You are not the first parent to explore money issues with your child from a position that acknowledges the need for ongoing personal growth, and you may rest assured that you will not be the last.

Do You Recognize, in Your Child, One of the Four Money Styles We Explored Earlier?

What should you do if you notice a potentially unhealthy money pattern emerging in your child, one that corresponds with one of the four styles you've read about earlier?

If your child shows an inordinate fascination with the idea of possession, and constantly seems to be saying things like, "It's mine," or, "I found it, I'm going to keep it," you may have a Keeper in the making. You need to convey the idea that real security comes from taking chances and learning that you can take care of yourself . . . even in a tough world. Talk about how you and your partner save for special goals such as retirement; by doing this, you let your child know the value of putting off gratification, and of being able to rely on yourself.

You can probably point your child's tendencies in a positive direction very easily. Encourage values such as thriftiness by teaching your child how to comparison shop and bargain hunt; he or she will probably take to the idea with little difficulty. Be consistent when it comes to money issues that affect your child. For example, give out the weekly allowance at the agreed-upon time. Make it clear that your child can rely on you in matters big and small. Try to demonstrate your own moderation in financial matters. Of course, you should also give your child plenty of love, affection, approval, and support. When you make an effort to demonstrate how pleased you are with your child, the chances of him or her wanting to please you again—and in the way you've just reinforced—are greatly increased.

If your child frequently says things like, "I'll buy something for you if you'll be my friend," you may have a budding Love Buyer. Teaching children that love is free can sometimes seem like a major challenge, but you must find a way to make it clear to your child that the true love he or she is after comes from being loved by parents, and not as a result of gifts or possessions received from you. It's the gleam in your eye that nurtures your child's self-esteem and teaches the feeling of being deserving, not the present you pass along.

Kids want your presence more than they want your presents. Make physical contact to show your support and approval. Give plenty of hugs to your child. Say how much you love him or her. Even parents with impossible schedules can manage this kind of positive reinforcement daily. A fast hug and kiss is better than an expensive gift with no real affection attached. Once you make this kind of regular connection with your child, it will become clear to him or her that love doesn't come with a price tag on it, and that the more your child gives it away, the more will come back in return. Saying "yes" to all requests for goodies may seem to keep peace in the household, and you may feel that the resulting calm represents your way of being loved, but following this path ultimately cripples children. They don't learn to prioritize, plan, put off gratification, or involve themselves in efforts to achieve an important goal. What's more, they don't appreciate things or people very much after a while, including you! Unless you are looking forward to being taken by a supremely jaded youngster, you must say "I love you" with your mouth, rather than your wallet.

Children who operate as Freedom Searchers may be motivated by a fear of dependency. They do what others want only until they no longer need anyone else, and then move briskly on to what pleases them. You can teach your child, hopefully by direct example, that those who have true independence are aware of what others think and can express themselves without fear of disapproval or of making others uneasy.

There's nothing wrong with an independent streak in your child, of course, but there's nothing wrong with considering the feelings of others, either. Demonstrate your own capacity to act compassionately and supportively with regard to your child's interests and passions, and you'll eventually see your child doing the same.

Parents who try to use the "power of the purse strings" as the primary means of influencing their children often find that their children exhibit the same Power Seeker behavior at the first opportunity. Not surprisingly, this often leads to bitter power struggles.

Children need to be taught that true power has more to do with being the person you want to be than it does with being able to use money and possessions to influence others. Reinforce what is unique and valuable about your child; praise a special talent or unique contribution. It's possible that your child will go through a period of intense interest with material objects, and will be fascinated by the status and respect certain possessions seem to carry. Try to demonstrate, by example, that you feel confident in your own ability to use money appropriately. That means pursuing sound plans for laudable goals—not purchasing in order to buy status, respect, or loyalty from someone else. Make it clear to your child that you understand that the kind of "power" associated with manipulation, punishment, withholding, and controlling is, ultimately, not any fun to wield.

A Few Thoughts on the Neglected Art of Saying "No"

You know you can't always get what you want, but do your kids know that? If not, then they need to hear it. It is very easy for children who grow up in a relatively affluent home to come to the conclusion that Mom and Dad generally get whatever they want. Why shouldn't the kids? After all, money spits out of machines in the wall these days—all it takes is a secret code. Sign a colored piece of paper, or hand over a plastic card, and the goods are cheerfully handed over. If adults sometimes seem to grab and buy whatever they want from the store shelves, is it that hard to understand why children expect to be able to do the same?

There will come a point in your child's life when it will make sense for you to explain that you—and most people—have to make choices when it comes to making purchases. Explain how you juggle expenses within your budget, how you and your mate make decisions together on major purchases, and how you forego some desirable things so you can afford to buy other, more essential items.

Saying "no" to your child can be surprisingly difficult. But everyone must learn to prioritize, to live with the reality of being unable to have whatever you want whenever you want it. Even if you can afford to give just about anything to your kids, you must recognize that, in the long term, they will be healthier persons if they have to put up with an occasional "no." Your child must learn to differentiate between needs and wants. It is your job to help make that distinction clear. If you fail to do so, you may be encouraging a skewed perspective.

Let your children know that their wish is not your command, regardless of how adamantly it is expressed. Encourage them to save or work for the big items that they want. Doing this helps build pride in accomplishment. Stress investment of time, effort, and personal involvement.

Are You Bribing Your Kids?

There is a big difference between a reward and a bribe, and you must make the distinction very clear to your child.

A child who goes above and beyond the call of duty, who does more than he or she was asked and expected to do, deserves a reward. If you must constantly manipulate your child into doing what you ask by offering rewards, however, you may be depriving your child of an opportunity to build self-esteem. He or she will feel resentful and will learn that to get what she wants, she has to do what you want first.

Money should not be tied to feelings of frustration or the need for reward. The best reward for your child is to show your appreciation and recognition without using money. Try a smile, a compliment on a job well done, and a few heartfelt words of thanks. If a child learns that material goods always accompany minimal levels of good behavior, there's a chance he or she will try to set up reward systems that match those of childhood. Compulsive spending may be the result.

Using money to reward good grades or punish poor ones can be a serious mistake. In fact, when money is the incentive, grades may actually decline because of the pressure to perform. Withholding an allowance for sub-par grades tells your child that money is power—your power over him or her. In all likelihood, the more you control the allowance, the more you will spark defiance. Parental recognition and pride, opportunities for greater independence, or both, are better ideas for motivating your child. There is an intrinsic value in performing a job well or doing well in school, and the sooner your child learns this lesson, the better he or she will perform.

Children need to learn that enjoying the process of learning is more important than a written grade. If you place too much emphasis on grades, you will risk teaching your child that the end justifies the means, and you may be applying the kind of pressure that encourages children to cheat to get the grade that will please you.

There are some forms of behavior that warrant withholding money, but they are few and far between. As a general rule, you are best advised simply to avoid money-related power struggles; these conflicts have an unfortunate way of delivering outcomes in which everyone loses. Pick the battles where the most critical no-nos may surface, such as your child stealing or buying drugs, to withhold money.

THE ALLOWANCE

Have you thought about why allowance is called an "allowance" instead of a "stipend," a "gift," or even "a dependent's small salary." What does the "allow" in allowance actually mean? The real point of an allowance is to allow your children to use money, and in the process gain confidence, independence, have fun, act like an adult—and, yes, make mistakes. An allowance can be the single best tool for teaching your children about sound money management. Handling this issue well will bring great benefits, not the least of which, of course, is avoiding your kids' daily demands for money. An allowance offers all sorts of learning experiences such as negotiating, problem-solving, researching, and money management.

When should you start giving your child an allowance? It's usually around age six that children can understand the values of coins, and no longer believe that a nickel should be more valuable than a dime because it's bigger. This is also around the time when they begin to handle money to ride the bus, buy lunch or a snack, or pay for small purchases themselves.

It is important that kids have some discretionary money, money that only they decide how to spend. It is also helpful to encourage kids to use some money for fun. Children as young as six or seven can start to learn about money with an allowance.

How much should you give? There's no easy answer. Talk with your child about his or her needs. Decide what things the allowance will cover. Talk about what your expectations are, how much the other kids get, and how people save for things that are important to them. Developing a mutually acceptable amount by means of a discussion along these lines is far more preferable than simply giving the child money when he or she asks for it! Doing that only teaches the child to ask for more. When parents follow the latter option, they often ask children to justify their need for money—or turn them down arbitrarily. In such situations, children may learn that the parent will always have the final say on whether or not particular expenditures are worthwhile. They will almost certainly have angry feelings about this state of affairs, feelings that they may or may not be able to be express easily.

To prevent money from sabotaging your relationship with your child, make sure that the process of handing over money is a loving and thoughtful one. The more you involve your child in a discussion of allowances, the better. Talk over the concept; get the child's ideas of what the allowance should cover. Ask if your child is willing to keep a daily diary of the kinds of expenses he makes; encourage him or her to make a bank as a rainy-day project; make a field trip to the bank together to see The Vault, and to talk to a bank officer about such things as where the money goes when someone gives it to the teller.

By raising the allowance by a dollar or so each birthday, your child will associate getting older with gaining more fiscal responsibility. Allowances should be given on a consistent basis, whether the child is good or bad. An allowance is neither a reward nor a punishment. The real world, as we all know, doesn't pay people to be good. Don't make your child ask for the allowance. You wouldn't like to ask for your paycheck, would you? Sunday night is a good time to give your child money for the week.

The allowance is your way of allowing your child the means to deal with the world on financial terms. It conveys the trust you have in him or her to handle something very important—money—and it lets your child know that you understand he or she will use it as it should be used, according to your agreement with him. Be sure to lay out the ground rules first, however. The most important point is that there will not be any advances on future allowances! You may want to consider helping out the first time your child goes over budget, but at that point you should probably make it clear that your child has to plan the best ways to spend, or save, the money so that it's there when important purchases have to be made. Then let your kids make their own mistakes with their money. Don't bail them out.

What about kids who aren't yet ready for an allowance? They can hand money to cashiers and storekeepers. They can play coin games to help them to learn to count. If they've inadvertently picked up some candy at the check-out counter and they haven't paid for it, help them learn that people need to choose between buying an item or replacing it.

Bank Accounts

Bank accounts are great tools for financial learning. Kids will get pleasure from seeing their savings grow, especially if the funds are earmarked for some item they want badly.

When my son was seven, he wanted a skateboard. I was not crazy about this particular toy, but I put him on a savings program anyway. I deviously hoped that it would take him so long to save the money, even with my matching funds, that he'd move on to something safer to play with.

I underestimated Eric. He went about pursuing this goal in earnest. He kept a running total of his holdings in his little money box and his custodial account at the local bank. Before too many months passed, we were doing some comparison shopping to get an idea of how much his skateboard might cost. Our trip to the biggest toy store in town was an exciting experience that had been preceded by months of anticipation and planning. Can you imagine the conclusions Eric would have reached if I'd told him that I'd changed my mind, and informed him that he wasn't really ready for the skateboard after all?

He dashed about the skateboard department and picked a red one that was in his price range. He bought it, held it on his lap all the way home, and tried all spring to master the thing. Thanks to persistence—and appropriate safety gear—he met with some success, and no broken bones.

My "matching funds" approach proved to be a very inspiring notion for Eric. I figured that if the federal government could get cities and states motivated to improve themselves by providing funds equal to those raised by taxes, I could help my son by doing something similar. Since kids don't make very much money, it can take forever to save enough to reach a goal. To improve the time element, and to provide an incentive to make some money through their own efforts, you may decide to match whatever your child socks away or earns. This doubles the amount in the bank, and makes the possibility of acquiring whatever the child wants more realistic. Kids will try harder to save money when they know that even small amounts saved will double.

Work, Work, Work . . .

The time will eventually come when you'll want to wean your child off of the weekly allowance and into the wonderful world of work.

It's best if your child works for someone other than you. That way, he or she will probably take orders better and make more of an effort to be responsible. After all, there'll be no wheedling the next-door neighbor for pay increases over the dinner table each night.

Don't start the process by tossing off suggestions. Talk about the jobs you may have performed when you were your child's age. Ask about what areas of employment would most interest your child. Offer to help out on the job search. If you do know of someone around the neighborhood who needs some help, clear it with your child first before making any contact. Remember that teenagers frequently experience parental help as interference and rebel against even well-intentioned gestures.

Some younger kids may relish the notion of becoming little entrepreneurs. Survey the toy box and bookcase with your child; pick out the excess, worn-out, and unwanted items. Most kids like stickers, so pass along a couple of sheets of labels of various colors; these are available at any stationery store, and will help you set your kid up in business in an updated version of the classic lemonade stand. Help your child assign prices for his old things, and make sure they're reasonable. Then pull out the old card table and set it up on the corner. Kids from the neighborhood may just buy; their parents may, too. Your child and you will love the extra space in his room, and you'll have passed along a lesson about the virtues of initiative (and recycling, for that matter). Your child will also benefit from knowing that the money earned by selling old belongings can go toward new, more exciting things—and if you match the profits, your entrepreneur will have a bundle of motivation, if not always a bundle of leftover cash, with which to spark the next venture.

Teach Kids to Give

Sharing is a learned activity. You understand the value of sharing by discovering the good feelings you get from giving to others. One way to instill generosity in kids is to encourage them to give to you while they're still young.

Let them buy you an apple, a gumball, or a can of soda while you're out on a shopping excursion. When you show your appreciation, your kids will find that giving feels good.

Another way to teach kids about sharing is by putting a "give-away box" in their closet. As they outgrow toys and clothes, you can ask your child to put the items in the box for other children who need them, but can't afford them. Take some things from the box to your church or synagogue, or the dentist's or pediatrician's office on your child's next visit. Leave them there for the other kids to play with and use. Occasionally giving small change to panhandlers when you're with your child will serve as a visible demonstration of the fortunate showing concern for the less fortunate.

Another trick is to encourage your child to be the one who puts the money into the donation plate or charity box at your church or synagogue. One family I know has a charity collection box in the kitchen. Everyone puts their extra change into it. This encourages the idea that charity is part of the family's value system.

Gift-giving deserves encouragement on any number of levels. During the holidays, make it clear that gifts don't have to be store-bought to be appreciated. In fact, since kids don't have much money, and you're stretched to the limit with your own gift list, handmade, homemade gifts are usually the very best option. Baking cookies for the whole family at special times of the year, and working together to make decorations and cards, can make for memories far more meaningful than those that flow from store-bought toys. By emphasizing creativity, resourcefulness, and making things by hand, you will help your children to learn to value their own skills.

Encourage your child to think of the recipient as someone special, and to customize the gift with that person in mind. While this requires time, patience, and planning, it also teaches your child thoughtfulness.

Peer Pressure

"But all the other kids have one!"

Peer pressure is probably the leading cause of arguments between parents and children. No matter what your socio-economic group, there always seems to be some family that's more bountiful in its gifts to its children than you are. Keeping up can be a terrific pain, and setting limits can be quite difficult.

Teens are acutely aware of themselves. They are in the process of discovering who they are and how they fit into their social scene. Their challenge during this teen time is to work through their need to be both dependent and independent. That's a tall order, and it usually doesn't come without angst . . . and the occasional cash infusion.

Peer pressure from fellow teens can create—and has created—multi-million dollar markets for everything from cars to video games. The under-lying messages of these products often promise teens respect, admiration, and self-enhancement. Even a parent who boasts of steely discipline can find it hard to say "no."

As parents, you want to be helpful and maintain peace in the home. But some parents may buy things for their teenage child as a substitute for spending time with the child. Parents may buy things for their teenagers in order to stifle a larger problem. Once in a while it's fine to indulge, and that's when it's appreciated. But the same basic guidelines about buying for younger children apply to teenagers. Too often, the financial sacrifices backfire. Set limits ahead of time—and stick to them.

Material things do make people feel good, but if possessions pass as self-esteem boosters, more and more money will be necessary to keep the good feeling going. Kids turn to externals to help them feel confident dur-ing the teen years. Athletic or academic success is surely one way for them to gain the recognition they crave, but having expensive clothing will do in a pinch, too. For a while.

So—What Do You Do About Your Teenager's Financial Issues?

Here are some tips that can make money issues less of a battleground, and make talking with teens less trying.

- When the time is right, have a discussion about such things as ownership, popularity, and how your teenager can make extra money.
- Convey your own values in a nonlecturing, nonjudgmental way.
- Don't ask too many questions. Try to make the ones you do ask thought-provoking, open-ended ones.
- Consider contributing something toward the desired item. (This beats paying for it outright, doesn't it?)

■ Remind your teenager that he or she has choices when it comes to spending money: fewer things for more money, or more things at less pricey stores.

■ Follow your instincts. If you have deep misgivings about a certain purchase, draw the line.

Kathie's daughter wanted new sheets and towels for college. After buying clothes, shoes, a computer, and knowing that books, monthly tuition payments, and bills for other "essentials" would be coming in, Kathie told her daughter that enough was enough. "You'll have to make do with the sheets and towels from home," she explained. It wasn't that the items in question cost a great deal of money. There had simply been no prior discussion about budgets. Kathie decided it was time to implement a change, and she did. It took a couple of heated discussions, but in the end Kathie knew she'd made the right decision.

Talking About Problems with the Family Finances

Discussing money openly with children can help them to feel more a part of the family's efforts. This is especially important in cases of divorce, layoff, or some other change with serious financial implications.

Knowing the general economic condition of the family may help the child avoid fantasizing and distorting the situation. Some kids, feeling desperation at home, actually pray that they will not require glasses or braces. Without the parent's guidance, some children fear that one more financial demand might cause a volcanic eruption.

It is impossible to hide the family's financial reality from children.

Kids pick up the household "vibes," whether or not you think they understand the content of your discussion. Explain the facts as best you can, in language the child will be able to understand. Point out that being in a family means being there for each other during the good times and the bad times.

If you don't take this step, you may be sowing the seeds of future money problems by encouraging your child to repress intense emotions, or engage in self-denial to avoid "rocking the boat." Such negative patterns may have serious repercussions well into your child's adult life.

Tell your child that yes, you have problems now, but you have a plan for the future. Explain it to him or her. Talk about how the family financial picture will affect him and what will be the same and what will be different in the near future. Let your child know that things will get better and that you have things pretty much under control. Let your child feel your hope, not your anxiety.

Chapter 12

Money and
Aging Parents

argaret lived in New York, her sister lived in Chicago, and their parents lived in New England. Their father was in his early 80s and their mother just turned 70. Both Margaret and her sister breathed sighs of relief that their parents seemed fine. Since they were so busy in their own lives, they were grateful that their parents could get along independently. However, Margaret's mother began calling her and complaining about her father's increasing disorientation. He would go out for a drive to the store and return hours later without any explanation. When Margaret asked her mother whether her father had gone to the doctor, her mother explained that he refused to even go to the local doctor. These phone conversations continued for a long time until Margaret finally took time off from work to spend a week with her parents and take her father for an examination at the regional medical center. Unfortunately, it turned out that he was in the early stages of Alzheimer's. Margaret then felt she had to get involved to figure out her parents' finances and begin looking into home health care options.

Margaret's hesitation to talk with her parents about their health and their finances until a crisis forced the issue is not unusual. Adult children often hesitate to ask their parents about estate issues, financial strategies during the parents' retirement years, and long-term care. However, in almost all cases, this hesitation must be overcome.

When you consider issues such as inheritance and old age with your mothers and fathers, it's natural for you to want to avoid exchanges that are likely to make you seem greedy or opportunistic. You may remember the family of money-hungry vultures hovering over Big Daddy in Tennessee Williams' classic *Cat on a Hot Tin Roof*; you may think to yourself that you must, whatever you do, not travel down that road.

Addressing such sensitive areas as whether or not in-home care or nursing homes will be an option, or what life-sustaining measures should be taken, may seem to be gauche and insensitive especially when your parents are clearly still robust and full of vitality. What child wants to be perceived as being more interested in a parent's decline and death than in his or her life?

Yet the period when your parents are soundest in mind and body is precisely the time you *must* address, tactfully and sensitively, the important financial issues that face them—and yourself. You may do yourself, and your parents, a serious disservice if you keep quiet out of denial in hopes that if you avoid the topic, your parents will not become infirm or die or superstition as though bringing up sensitive issues will only serve to bring "bad luck."

Your parents will someday pass away, and the period before they do is likely to be a difficult and trying one for everyone. Talking about this period may be difficult, but it is nowhere near as difficult as facing the circumstances in question without any prior planning whatsoever.

Although it's sometimes difficult to talk with parents about the financial situation they will face in later years, or to plan how best to offer them the help and support they may need, it is not impossible as long as the discussion takes place while they are still healthy and rational.

To be sure, asking how much money your parents have can be a touchy undertaking. Is it possible you'll be told, directly or indirectly, to mind your own business? Yes. The subjects of aging, infirmity, and mortality are hard for everyone to broach. Yet, with a sensitive approach, you can make it clear that you are interested not in how much money you will receive after the funeral, but in the serious responsibility you face taking care of your parents and their estate.

In many cases, parents are relieved beyond words for the opportunity to share their thoughts about these issues with their children. There's a very good chance your parents have been trying, with some difficulty, to avoid talking with you about these issues because of their concern for you. Most parents are uneasy about burdening or worrying their children with financial issues. By sensitively taking the initiative and raising some of the most important questions yourself, you may be able to remove a heavy weight from your parents' minds by demonstrating that your love and concern for them will extend even to the difficult questions they will face later in life.

How to Address Sensitive Financial Issues with Your Parents

Here are some strategies that will help you address the important financial issues you and your parents are likely to face as they grow older.

- Raise the issue in your parents' home, rather than your own. They're likely to be more comfortable in their own territory.

- Begin by asking general, nonthreatening questions about their activities. Are your parents planning a vacation in the near future? If they have not yet retired, are one or both of your parents planning to work part-time after retirement? By raising such issues, you can gradually move toward talking about their own financial preparations for their later years. Don't lecture them. Express concern by saying something like, "I'd like to know what your thoughts are for your financial well-being. This is not so much for me, but because I want to be sure you're going to be okay."

- Consider mentioning your own will (you should have one). If you have thoughts or questions on preparing or revising your will, your parents might have valuable advice. If you have specific requests you'd like your parents to know about in case you die before they do, such as their taking responsibility for raising one or more of your children, this could open the door to discussions of other types of planning.

■ Always make it clear that your interest is in your parents' security, safety, and happiness, rather than your own financial status.

Once You've Got the Ball Rolling . . .

You will want to clarify the most important information about your parents' financial plans. The best time to do this is probably when your parents have started to contribute as much as you do, or more, to the conversation. If you're doing most of the talking, that may be a sign that they're uncomfortable dealing with the issue, or have doubts about your motives. Keep focusing on general, nonthreatening issues, and try to get your parents to start talking about their own plans and concerns. When in doubt, ask what, if anything, they're worried about when it comes to the financial situation they face. Then listen.

If you're able to, find out what the assets are, and where they're located. Ask about safe deposit boxes and insurance policies, too. Are there any debts you should be aware of? What sources of income do your parents have? Get the names of their advisors—accountant, stockbroker, insurance agent, attorney. Find out if your parents have adequate health insurance. Ask whether they've thought about moving to a smaller home or to a more hospitable climate.

Once you get this far, you will have made great headway. Don't try to cover everything in one discussion. If time allows, deal with more serious issues at a later time. Those topics could include:

■ What to do in the event of incapacity.

■ What your parents expect when it comes to day-to-day care during their frail years. If their plans include you, listen first, and consider your response before you react in any way. If their plans include medical or nursing care, consider volunteering to do the research necessary to find out how their financial situation match up with the current or likely costs of such care.

■ Whether or not a joint checking account is in order.

■ How to coordinate contacts with a family attorney who will help you deal with questions relating to trusts, estate planning, and power of attorney.

■ Where the most important documents (such as property and burial deeds) are to be found.

Good Reasons to Talk About Estate Planning

Money is, as a general rule, difficult to talk about. Death is even more so. When you address issues related to estate planning with your parents, diplomacy, tact, and forbearance are the orders of the day.

Focus first on how the various responsibilities of administering the estate are going to be handled. You should try to establish the answers to these questions in consultation with a trusted attorney who is skilled in dealing with estate matters. Beyond that, you and your parents may—or may not—be comfortable discussing specific inheritance issues.

The advantages to knowing who's getting what well ahead of time can be significant. Siblings who receive differing amounts of money or property may be able to head off years of misunderstanding and resentment if they have the opportunity to discuss these sensitive decisions with the parents who make them. If your parents have decided to try to compensate for someone's lower earning potential by giving that person a greater share of the assets, it may be helpful for all who are affected by this choice to be able to deal openly with their parents on this issue.

Then there's the matter of sound long-term planning. Important financial decisions are more likely to be made intelligently when there is time to prepare for them. Unfortunately, many an adult child has made a poor set of choices immediately after receiving a substantial and, often, unexpected sum of money from a parent's estate. Discussing the details of inheritance issues early on may help you or others avoid sudden, ill-advised spending sprees, or keep you from making financial choices motivated by guilt at having received more money than someone else did. The best reason to spend a vast chunk of your inheritance money on a lavish vacation is that it makes sense for you and your family to do so, not because of your long-simmering anger at your mother for years of mistreatment. The best reason to give a lot of money to charity is that you believe in its mission, not because you have a sense of having received something you didn't deserve.

Those are the two chief benefits of addressing inheritance issues directly with your parents. By the same token, however, it certainly isn't in anyone's interest to demand a full accounting from parents who have determined that it would be best to avoid revealing their bequests while they are still alive. If you can find an appropriate way to encourage your parents to discuss their objectives for making certain estate choices, do so. If you can't, don't pressure them. You'll probably shut down lines of communication and perhaps encourage volatile exchanges that will only make future heartache more acute.

Unspoken Concerns

One of the most common concerns parents have about leaving large amounts of money to their children has to do with motivation. Will their adult children simply goof off for the rest of their lives? Will they spend the money unwisely? Will they become spoiled, and sleepwalk through their adulthood, feeling that they're somehow entitled to easy lives? In other words, will the money do more harm than good?

Many of these parents recall their own early struggles to earn a living, and wonder in hindsight whether making things easier for their own children was really the best thing they could have done. They conclude, usually with some justification, that the process of struggling, sacrificing, and working to reach important goals had a profoundly positive effect on their own lives. While their own children may have grown into fine adults, these parents often wonder about the overall impact financial advantages made on their children. It's important to understand these thought processes as you assess the decisions your parents make, or made, in dividing up their estate.

Trust is a major message in a will. Even when parents have a trusting relationship with their children, they may elect to put off the distribution of it to allow the adult children to learn how to manage it.

You should understand, too, that some Power Seeker parents expect that their adult children will use inherited money exactly as they direct.

Such parents may have made a habit, for instance, of bestowing "strings-attached" gifts to their children over the years. The father may have provided funds to buy a house for an adult child, in return for a "say" in where the house was located, how it was furnished, and how much money should be spent on landscaping. Such gifts have been known to lead to serious psychological problems on the part of the recipient, whose own self-image and sense of personal ability may suffer in such a domestic situation. The impact of "strings-attached" gifts can be even more devastating when they are incorporated within the legal confines of a will.

For example, a deeply religious parent might state that a certain sum is to be used only for the grandchildren's religious education. This attempt at control might be the result of anger or disappointment that the adult child didn't follow a religious path. Of course, the feelings in this type of situation can be complicated, and would probably include bitterness and loss of love.

A will is more than a statement of how assets are to be divided among heirs. It can say a lot about the parent-child relationship. Daughters, for instance, may be treated much differently than sons. Even in these days of college-educated daughters with businesses of their own, parents may still turn to their sons to carry out the estate responsibilities. This, of course, is their choice, but it may be the cause of some resentment or hurt feelings on your part. Remember that your parents are acting in accordance with their own value systems, which are not necessarily identical to yours. Try to deal with difficult problems in a constructive manner—and don't be afraid to seek out professional help in dealing with what you perceive to be unfairness.

If doing so in a tactful, sensitive way is possible, having discussions about how the family money is to be disbursed may dramatically improve the parent-child relationship. Talking about your parents' needs, and your own career decisions, values, and expectations, can draw you all closer together. Try to share your own feelings about the impact the family money could have on your own growth, family life, friendships, and intimacies. Respect your parents' objectives and desires, follow their lead when you can do so in good conscience, and remember that honest communication usually strengthens relationships—even when there is disagreement.

Chapter 13

Friends and Money

*S*usan and Debbie have been friends since junior high. They've
managed to stay in touch despite living in different cities and
*having very different lifestyles. Debbie is happily married and has one
child. Susan is single and, though she has a fair job, is more concerned with buying clothes and living it up on vacation. In the past,
they've usually split expenses when they ate out or went to the theater.
Now, however, Susan has been asking Debbie to pick up the tab when
they do things together. Initially, Susan was almost casual—she was
short on cash that week and would pick up the check next time—but
in reality she "forgets" to do so. Debbie is starting to resent Susan's
behavior. After all, although Debbie's husband works, they have many
expenses. Debbie wonders why Susan can't manage her own money
better. On the other hand, she doesn't want to jeopardize the relationship by telling Susan her feelings.*

Should you loan money to a friend? Should you borrow money from a
friend?

Whether you're the borrower or the lender, the subject of loans between friends can be an uncomfortable one. Closely evaluating your own
motivation is an important part of the process of making mature decisions
on this score—and, indeed, of making choices regarding any aspect of
money as it affects your relationships with friends.

> The best time to ask for a loan is also the best time to offer one: When the money's appearance is likely to do more good than harm for one or preferably both of the people involved.

The Right Reasons to Lend Money

The wish to help out a friend is certainly at the top of the "right reason" list. But how constructive is that help going to be?

Think of parents who "help their children out" by loaning them the money they need to get into a first home. While there is a certain altruism at work here, perhaps a good investment, there's also a very practical consideration that may be motivating such parents. In many situations, they are eager to get the kids out of their own house! Buying the new home represents a benefit for both sides. The same basic objective may underlie a loan intended to help a child start a new business: If the business succeeds, the child won't have to keep asking for money. In both cases, if there's a written plan for repayment and/or a discussion of what will happen if the loan can't be repaid as expected, there's probably a decent chance for a positive outcome for both sides.

You should ask yourself whether or not your situation with a friend—either as a borrower or a lender—has the potential for a similar, mutually beneficial impact; it has to be one that lets both people feel they're doing the right thing.

Helping a friend deal with a genuine emergency, for instance, may be one good reason to lend money. Your friend gets to deal with the problem at hand; you get to show the support you hope your friend would display if the situation were reversed. If the loan doesn't represent a constant, unhealthy pattern that inhibits growth, both sides can feel they've dealt with things in a mature and caring way.

The Wrong Reasons to Lend or Borrow Money

If you're considering loaning money to make up for guilt over prior misdeeds, or for guilt about earning more than your friend does, stop. If you're appealing for money as the result of a similar unspoken agenda, stop. There's probably going to be a problem. Guilt is not a great foundation on which to build a strong relationship.

> If you find yourself saying, "I should really loan my friend this money," that's probably an indicator that you're harboring internal doubts that need to be addressed. If you know something is the right thing to do, you don't lecture yourself that you "should" do it. Focus not on what you should do, but what you feel good about doing.

I have two rules of thumb that I use with my patients in therapy. The first is to check out the reality of the situation. Think of all the real aspects and consider such things as true feelings, what you want to do, what you don't want, and what might happen if you don't come through. The worst-case scenario probably won't come true. If, for example, you fear losing your friendship if you don't do what your friend wants, reflect on how to keep the friendship and convey this wish to your friend. Friendships based on doing what someone wants aren't worth having. The other rule of thumb is to not hurt your Self. Yes, Self has a capital S in this case; it refers to the most precious part of you, and you must guard it. If you simply can't afford to loan money, or if doing so will cause you financial or emotional pain, forget it.

The Keeper Hates Loans

Most Keepers don't like to loan money. They experience loans as having something taken away from them. The Keeper's goal is to accumulate money, not to give it away. Deep down, they don't expect loans ever to be repaid, so they fear and avoid them. Keepers aren't particularly generous people.

Keepers who do lend money may count off the days until they are supposed to get the funds back—and share the countdown with all the relevant parties. They do a great job of making friends and family feel guilty for asking them for money in the first place, and they make people feel even more guilty if there are problems with repayment. Many older Keepers have short-term memory problems, but somehow display elephant-like long-term retention when money is the issue.

These people want you to think of them as martyrs because of all the sacrifices they make for you. They are often very angry at the world.

The Love Buyers Love Loans

A good many Love Buyers try to prove their own lovability by getting money from people. Their unspoken (or spoken) message: "If you really love me, you'll lend me the money."

Love Buyers who agree to make loans are often out to prove how generous they are so they can bask in the appreciation and supposed affection of the recipient. Some Love Buyers who really can't afford to meet their own expenses have been known to make quite extravagant loans, simply to show off their beneficent nature. They fear that if they refuse to lend money, they will lose a friendship. Not surprisingly, they often lose both the money and the "friends" in question.

Power Seekers Have Chains, Not Strings, Attached to Loans

Some Power Seekers will loan you money and then believe they have a right to control your life. They thoroughly abuse their role as lenders.

Initially, they'll want to know all the details of your need for the money. Then they'll make "suggestions" about how you should spend the money they're about to pass along. All too often, those "suggestions" turn into unhealthy domination of various aspects of your life.

Not all Power Seekers follow this pattern, but those who do are worth avoiding. If you seem to be facing an inquisition before the money is passed along, or if you have heard stories about how previous loan situations with this person have turned sour, you're probably better off heading to a bank, even if it means paying a little extra money. Lending cash ought not give power to the lender to make all (or any) of the decisions. Power Seekers fear losing control, so having a clear understanding about their expected level of involvement in your affairs is a good idea.

Freedom Searchers Take It Easy

Freedom Searchers who are in a position to loan money are perhaps the easiest of the four groups to borrow from. Loaning them money, however, can be problematic.

Elongated or "creative" repayment patterns are common among Free-dom Searchers. These people are, you will remember, deeply suspicious about encumbrances, entanglements, and commitments. They like to do things on their own terms, and that often extends to repaying money they borrow. If you're considering loaning money to a Freedom Searcher, think twice about your own motives and that of your friend. In the event that you decide to extend the loan, you should seriously consider setting up a formal written agreement. You should establish such an agreement with any friend when loaning a large amount of money, but when it comes to Freedom Searchers, formal terms for even modest amounts should prob-ably be set down in black and white.

Saying No

Telling a friend that you've decided not to lend him or her money can sometimes be very tricky. The best approach is to share, tactfully, your true feelings with your friend, and to make it clear that you've given the matter a good deal of consideration.

You may want to say something like, "I've slept on this question, and while you might not understand all of the things that I went through in considering it, please know that I have given it very serious thought. I just don't think it would be in our best interests to do this together. And listen, just because I won't be lending you this money doesn't mean that I don't want to help you think this problem through. Maybe I can help you in a different way."

Once you say something like this, you and your friend have a problem to think over. It's not just the friend's problem, it's yours, too—and that can be extremely helpful. Perhaps you can come up with some new ideas, or point your friend toward some contact who may be helpful.

Income Disparities and Work Commitments

Large differences in income between friends often cause a change in the friendship on a practical level. Consider Amy and Ellen's case. These two were college roommates; after they graduated, they lived in the same city, but went on to quite different jobs. Amy is now a teacher earning thirty thousand dollars a year; Ellen works for an investment banking firm and earns eighty thousand. Realistically speaking, Amy can't join the health club Ellen belongs to, and she can't make too many trips to the white-tablecloth restaurants her friend prefers.

If you have a relationship with a friend that reminds you of Amy and Ellen's, you will need to find some way to make the necessary adjustments—especially if you are the one with less money to spend. If you let your friend know what your budget is, and suggest a few places you're comfortable visiting when she calls up suggesting that you get together, she'll probably follow your lead. Similarly, if you take the initiative and invite her to trek through a museum exhibit or some other moderately priced event with you, you can probably both have a great time without spending too much money.

Friendships can fall by the wayside temporarily when workplace demands arise. If you've fallen out of touch because of a hectic work schedule, tell your friends that you are inundated with work-related things and that you will be scarce—for a while—because of business commitments. Your friend probably won't take it personally or think that you're making money a more important priority than people—if you make it clear that the reason for placing the call in the first place is that you value your friendship. Without that communication, your friend could indulge in some unfortunate speculation: "You're too busy to call? I must not be good enough to be your friend anymore."

Even with the best of "let's keep in touch" intentions, work-related commitments can lead to significant changes in a relationship. You tend to outgrow friends when mutual needs disappear. What's interesting is that the feelings toward these people usually remain, and the friendships can often be picked up more or less from where they left off, assuming that you and your friend want to pick them up.

While it's common to talk about work-related crises, hectic schedules, and money in general with friends, you don't usually discuss your thoughts and feelings about significant income differences between yourself and those who are close to you. It's easy to complain about taxes or the cost of living, but talking about one's personal financial situation can be uncomfortable, even among people of similar income levels. If it's awkward under those circumstances, it can be downright threatening to many people who earn a good deal more (or less) than their friends.

FRIENDS AND MONEY   **179**

People who are struggling to make ends meet may find that resentment is a real issue in their relationships with more affluent friends. And while many people may wish they had the "problem" of earned or inherited wealth, these individuals probably don't know the extent of the self-doubt, guilt, and other negative feelings such money can give rise to in one's social dealings with others. One's friends often express (or feel, but don't express) jealousy; questions of whether or not one is being taken advantage of may arise. Open communication about key issues is, as usual, the best remedy—but it's worth bearing in mind that significant income differences may represent a problem that some friendships simply can't accommodate.

People Who Can't Accept Help

There are some people who cannot accept help, financial or otherwise, even if that help is desperately needed and offered in a loving, non-controlling way.

These people typically have trouble accepting gifts of any kind; they invariably offer the response, "Oh, you shouldn't have." What's disconcerting is that they obviously really mean it. After recovering from the nonplused reaction of such acquaintances after passing along a present, many vow never to give them anything ever again.

These are usually people who want to maintain their sense of independence, since they fear being obligated to, or dominated by, others. They can't tell the difference between help that's offered out of true concern and that which is presented out of a desire to control. (In their background, there may have been no way to distinguish between these two types of help.) Consequently, these people would much prefer to be the giver than the receiver. That way, they are in the more powerful position: They give when they want and how much they want, and they are beholden to no one.

Generally, these "gift-challenged" types can manage quite well on their own, and they want you to know it. Their needs are small and their wants aren't many. You won't hear many complaints from these people, nor will they make a habit of whining or criticizing. They take good care of themselves, and they virtually never take advantage of others. The truth is, they don't take much of anything!

Some of these people are depressed and deeply insecure. Their prickliness tends to keep others at a safe—but lonely—distance. While they may have friends, the terms are usually quite strict: The relationship is based on the principle of minding one's own business, rather than on sharing. It's hard, in other words, to have a heart-to-heart talk with these folks. It's usually a major challenge to be loving with them, because they may thoughtlessly rebuff even the most basic gestures of caring.

It's a good bet that during childhood, there were many reasons for these people to believe that their most important needs were not going to be met. They probably experienced great insecurity and were deeply disappointed by someone very close to them. Over time, they learned to lower their expectations—or abandon them altogether. They may call themselves "survivors." They often feel that since they made it through a trying time alone, they don't really need anyone or anything now.

> If you have difficulty accepting even modest gifts, simple person-to-person assistance, or short-term financial help from others, there's a good chance that you are needlessly distancing the other people in your life, and short-changing yourself when it comes to your relationships with friends.

It is possible for a non-taking person to change. If you are one, the first baby step to take is to remind yourself that you are no longer a child. As an adult, you can evaluate your situation with caution, not distrust. You don't have to say, "No, thanks" to everything in order to survive.

Make an effort to find—and acknowledge—things that you truly like about yourself. Are you precise? (That's a better word than "picky.") Do you get a lot done on your own? (That's a better way to look at your work style than declaring yourself to be a "loner." Make a list of such positive qualities on paper; review it regularly.

Creative Ways to Offer Help

Margo knew that her friend Cindy couldn't afford the computer course she needed to help her improve her skills for an upcoming job hunt. Instead of offering her money outright, Margo called a few of their mutual friends—and together, they chipped in for the tuition. Not all the friends gave the same amount of money. (Actually, Margo contributed most of it.) The result, though, was that Cindy was able to recognize the gift as an act of love, rather than as a symbol of indebtedness. Margo was gratified too, since she was able to show her care for her friend without assuming total responsibility for the gift.

I recently heard of a group of close friends who took a particularly creative approach to the task of establishing a certain amount of common financial security; they made contributions to a pool of money reserved for emergencies—and accessible to all members of the group. The pool started out with $6,000, and each month the members added $5 per person, per family. If anybody needed less than $50 during any given week, that amount could be withdrawn without consulting anyone. For sums over $50, the group met and discussed the request. The system worked amazingly well. One high-income member of the group, who had been concerned that he would end up contributing more than anyone else to the fund, turned out, for a while, to be the one who withdrew the most from the fund. After he was laid off, he had the biggest bills to cope with!

This fund brought all the members of the group a sense of security. It represented a way to help friends out, and be helped in turn, without having to stir up the emotions that inevitably accompany asking a friend for money. This group developed and implemented a superb idea, one that many other groups of friends would do well to adapt.

The Restaurant Check

Who picks up the restaurant tab when friends go out? This nearly universal issue is worth discussing in detail. In many settings, the right to pay for a restaurant meal is seen as a symbol of personal power and prestige. When two people who think this way hook up with one another, they may stage an impressive, drawn-out battle over who's going to be paying for the meal. That battle may only end when one of the participants wins the right to pay the tip—and a promise that he or she will, without fail, be allowed to pick up the tab next time.

Such power issues may be at work in your interactions with a friend. Let's say your friend is a Power Seeker who earns three times as much as you do. If she invites you to a fine restaurant and assures you that it's her treat, you might feel some initial reservations, but might eventually agree to the outing and have a fine time. But what if your friend not only picks the restaurant, but also tells the maitre d' where you both want to sit? What if she drops broad hints about what you should order, and then instructs you as to how it should be eaten? What if she makes a point of emphasizing how expensive everything was before she pays the bill? In such a situation, you may end up feeling as though you're a child being told what to do. Such a friend is using money to say, "I need your submissiveness."

The real question is not "Who's picking up the check?" but "How comfortable are you with this situation?" Most of us are quite content to make do with the common practice of dividing the check up in a mutually agreeable way, but sometimes there's a trade-off worth making when other options present themselves. The friend who seems so powerful may, in fact, be quite needy. For example, she may want you to listen to her latest hard-luck story . . . and offer some advice. When she treats you to a fancy dinner, perhaps she's showing her sincere appreciation for all your expertise and support. If you have no problem with this "transaction," you may decide that alternating between your friend's choices of restaurants and your own, with each person acting as "host" for the meal in question, makes sense.

Jealousy and Envy

If a friend told you that she was preparing for a trip around the world—a trip you couldn't afford—would you be jealous . . . or envious? The difference between these two emotions is often misunderstood.

Jealousy focuses on something of value (or someone you love). When you are jealous, you suspect someone or something has been stolen or is about to be taken from you. You may have felt jealousy if your lover turned to another person, for instance, or if someone beat you out of a promotion.

Envy is a much bigger, meaner, all-consuming, and self-destructive emotion. Envy means resenting someone else's good fortune. When someone else has more, does better, or receives more, it seems to the envious person that there's less in the way of achievement, recognition, or reward available for him or her. Another person's happiness, even if it is completely unrelated to the world in which the envious person operates, is bad news.

Deeply envious people are rarely, if ever, pleased by positive developments in the lives of others. They're upset that these positive developments did not take place in their own lives. Chronic envy feeds on life's inequities; according to the envious, some people seem to have "all the luck" and get more than their "fair share" of the bounties in life. Those who let envy consume them are trapped in a permanent cycle of complaint and resentment, since there are always people who are richer, more successful, happier, or more attractive than they are. Jealousy generally passes away; deep envy can be a sign of a serious long-term imbalance in our interactions with others. Since it's based on the erroneous idea that there's only a limited amount of love, happiness, and good fortune to go around, it leads to a skewed perspective.

A secure friend who is not the envious type can be happy for you if you're lucky enough to be able to enjoy a trip around the world—even if she can't afford the trip herself. She may ask you to send her a postcard so she can take part in your experience—and she may enjoy seeing pictures of things she may never be able to see on her own. There could be some initial tension over such a situation in even the best of friendships, but a well-adjusted friend will work through them, perhaps by means of a little humor. ("Well, it's too bad we won't be able to enjoy St. Moritz together— I'm already booked on the Jersey Shore that week.")

Ironically, envy is less about others than it is about anger at one's own life. (Envy is also a way of avoiding taking action to address how we feel about anger.) Envy is passive and, very often, utterly draining. It takes a lot of energy to keep going. Envy is a net loss, because it uses up attention without inspiring us to change or improve our lot in any way.

If you feel yourself reacting in an envious way to good news about other people—good news that has no direct relation to your own situation—you should ask yourself, "What am I really envious of? And how can I get some of that for myself?" You could use the answers to get in touch with what you feel is missing from your life (a sense of adventure and spontaneity, perhaps), and work up some realistic strategies for how to get it. If it's a sudden, unexpected journey you're after, you should find a way to make that happen. You may conclude that it doesn't have to be a trip through China after all, and that a romantic weekend with your mate at a local bed-and-breakfast inn will fill the gap you've identified.

Part V

The Power Brokers

Chapter 14

When Your Ex Is Part of Your Support

$\mathcal{S}$ ally and Jeff had been married for nine years and had two children. Although the couple had problems occasionally, neither one anticipated the end of their marriage. However, when Jeff's job began to require more and more travel, leaving Sally home alone with the children, the relationship deteriorated. Jeff paid less attention to what was happening at home and Sally turned to spending to alleviate some of the stress she felt. Not only did she redecorate the house and buy the kids a playroom full of new toys, she began taking tennis lessons. By the time the two split up and prepared to divorce, their finances were in terrible shape. Now, Sally faces an uncertain future as she has to decide whether to sell the house, and go back to work all while worrying over whether Jeff will keep up his payments of child support and limited alimony.

Sally's increased spending prior to her divorce isn't unusual. When money is all that's left of a relationship, often the most extreme elements of each partner's money style kick in—with unfortunate consequences for all involved. Power Seekers may withhold everything they can in an attempt to control the situation. Love Buyers who feel their self-esteem plummeting may run up credit card bills. Keepers may hoard a stash of cash ("just in case." Freedom Searchers may leave material things behind and run for their lives.

Whatever your own initial style may be and whatever steps you take to channel it constructively, you will eventually come to a point when you realize that since you are on your own, you will have to be the one who plans for your financial future. While you may be getting financial support from your ex-spouse now, it's important to plan for the time when you will be independent. In addition, because you may be primarily responsible for yourself and your children, it's also important to prevent needless fights with your ex and get on with your life.

Taking charge of your own finances is central to your well being.

Free at Last

If you've had little or no experience in handling your own money, the post-breakup period can be both frightening and liberating.

New experiences can always be a little intimidating at first, but many women in this situation come to rejoice in their newfound freedom to spend what they want, when they want. Even if you don't have much money, you will probably breathe a sigh of relief when you realize that there's no one around to offer opinions on what you eat, where you go, or whether or not something is too expensive or too frugal. Your opinions are the ones that matter now. Choices must still be made responsibly, of course, but if you have spent years trying, perhaps unsuccessfully, to accommodate your spouse's money outlook and your own, having real independence when it comes to spending money may feel new and exciting. You can decide to eat at home for a month so you can save money to buy something special for yourself or your kids. It's your choice!

A word of advice, though: If the thrill of independence comes about solely as a result of money you receive from your ex-spouse, you should consider finding some type of work so that you can start spending or saving money of your own, too. Women who can earn money are more self-confident than those who haven't received their own paycheck, and their self-esteem is usually higher, too. As a result, they're in a better position to adjust to their new lives.

Even if you're working, however, you should prepare yourself for the likely arrival of lower living standards and other obstacles.

Lower Living Standards

After a divorce, you can count on the living standards of both ex-spouses going down. In most cases, the double expenses associated with residences, vehicles, utilities, and any number of other budget items make it impossible to retain exactly the standards you enjoyed during marriage, even if both spouses are now working, and only one did before.

Even with a new job and financial help from your ex, you may find that you have to make some changes, such as living in a less desirable neighborhood, driving a used car, or vacationing bed-and-breakfast style instead of at a top-notch hotel. The court system tries to find equitable solutions for mothers and children, since mothers are still the likely custodial parent, but the system must also acknowledge the reality that men have to have enough money to live a decent life, too. If the courts attempt to impose an unfair arrangement on a man who is the primary source of income for his ex-wife and children, there's a very real chance the former husband will lose all motivation to work—or he may skip town and leave no forwarding address.

What about after the initial transition to independent life? Women with children generally have to continue to make do with less, often because they are trying to maintain a home and go to school or work. Men recover from the financial shock of divorce more quickly, and their post-divorce incomes tend to rise over time. Of course, men as a group still earn more, have higher social security benefits, get better health care from their place of employment, and sock away more money for retirement than women do.

In other words, the odds are against you.

Divorced women must take the best possible care of themselves financially if they hope to overcome the "structural" financial obstacles they face, obstacles they probably didn't face as married women.

The days of huge alimony settlements are probably over, due largely to the emergence of women as viable wage-earners. The focus today is on child support payments, and in many cases you shouldn't count on getting much of that. Even non-working wives with children frequently get as little as 10 to 15 percent of the husband's take-home pay, and working wives get relatively little support unless they've been married a long time.

If you're negotiating or even contemplating a divorce, it's up to you to provide as much documentation as possible detailing the high cost of raising kids today. Receipts from doctors, dentists, summer camps, clothing stores, and book and record stores will all be helpful. You should also collect as many pertinent financial documents as you can. Old tax returns, insurance bills, car payments, bank accounts and credit card statements can all demonstrate your family's lifestyle and let the court know exactly where the assets are to be found. (Many a soon-to-be-ex-husband has dragged his heels when it comes to providing this kind of material.)

Divorce is often a painful, drawn-out process featuring raw emotions and tattered nerves, one that involves the former partners in bitter "win/lose" struggles. Divorce also involves lawyers, which means that in addition to being a painful process, it's usually an expensive one. Attorneys still get a big chunk of the money that's being argued over as they wrangle to try to win what they can for their clients. "Winning" is nice, and it may help to heal some emotional pain, but there are times when it comes at too high a cost. If your ex-husband is going to be providing you and/or your children with support for some time in the future, there's something to be said for negotiating shrewdly, but keeping personal recrimination to a minimum.

"How Do I . . . ?"

Some women emerging from a failed marriage are novices when it comes to performing such tasks as balancing a checkbook or filling out an income tax return. Perhaps you have to buy a car, negotiate a mortgage, and start a retirement account, all for the first time—and all while you're still reeling from the considerable emotional stress of the divorce. These can be daunting jobs indeed.

Here are some tips that can help you keep your mental health during the transition stage.

■ Maintain an optimistic attitude. Reinforce your internal conviction that you can do what needs to be done.

- Remember that you are an adult, not a child. You are on your own now, so you must take the very best care of yourself. No one else can do this for you!

- Ask for help if you need it. Consider appealing to friends, parents, siblings, or coworkers.

- Make a list of the things you need to do. Break each chore down to manageable parts. "See" each step of the chore so you can visualize that it is, in fact, doable.

- Prioritize the chores so you don't feel overwhelmed. Focus on one task at a time and try to finish what you set out to accomplish.

- Talk to yourself kindly and reassuringly throughout your challenging experiences.

Money Games Men Play

If you are supposed to receive monthly amounts of money from your ex, you may find receiving the actual payments something of an unpleasant adventure. Insecure ex-husbands who control the money in such situations have been known to abuse their power quite brazenly in an attempt to frighten, hurt, and manipulate former partners.

Some men withhold funds long enough to convince their ex-wives to undergo the additional expense of hiring a lawyer and covering initial court fees in order to collect the money owed. As a general rule, these men generally assume that such a step is too expensive and complicated for their ex-wives to consider seriously. Sometimes they're right; sometimes they're wrong.

It's worth remembering that the courts are likely to be on your side when it comes to helping you receive the agreed-upon amounts of money. Going back to court may be a time-consuming process, but if things have deteriorated to the point where your ex is making no attempt whatsoever to meet his obligations, it may be your best option. Rest assured that your former mate will get the message about his responsibility, since he'll almost certainly have to spring for attorney fees and deal with the judge, who's not likely to be pleased with the situation. If your ex is on salary and has missed several payments, the court can attach his earnings. This will probably embarrass him enough to encourage him to mend his ways.

Embarrassment can be a powerful motivator. In fact, before you head back to the courtroom, you may want to consider contacting someone within your former spouse's family. By appealing to that person, you may be able to shame your ex-husband into paying up. Many of the men who play money games, however, couldn't care less about what members of their family think.

It's important to try to understand the reason your ex withholds your money. Is he truly financially overburdened, or is he simply out to cause you pain and suffering? If you're looking at the former situation, try to show some understanding, and keep hostile exchanges to an absolute minimum. Make every effort to avoid becoming an enemy. Enemies don't get paid.

If you have custody of the children, remember that your ex-husband is more likely to pay you on a regular basis if he gets a chance to see his kids. Do not attempt to use the children as bargaining chips.

It may be tempting to withhold visiting privileges from a dad who doesn't pay up, but this strategy usually backfires. A better way to handle things is to state honestly and straightforwardly the effect your ex-husband's behavior had on his children's feelings. You could say something like, "Mary was disappointed that she couldn't buy her friend the toy she wanted, and Joey was angry that he had to stay home last Saturday night since he didn't have enough money to go out with his friends for pizza and the movies. Things are tight around here when you don't make payments on time."

There's a very good chance your ex truly wants to avoid hurting the children you both brought into the world. This is an interest you both share, and shared interests are the basis of workable agreements. Remind your ex-husband that even though you both have strong emotions to deal with, the welfare of your children comes first. While it may be hard to be polite to someone who has been the cause of bitter disappointment, it's worth trying to do so if only to convey the message that your ex-husband is still needed as a supportive father, both emotionally and financially.

Even if he is on your "hit list," your children probably still see him as their hero. Accept that fact and work from there.

Anger Is an Expensive Emotion

Emily didn't get anywhere near the amount of money she expected from her divorce settlement. Even though she had signed off on the amount that her ex-husband had committed to pay, and even though she was the one who had wanted out of the marriage, she harbored some deep resentments. Emily had been raised to believe that being married meant being taken care of—forever. When events disproved this assumption, she spent a good deal of time and energy being furious.

After her divorce, Emily's friends noticed that she had developed a new habit of chewing intently on her lower lip and cheek. She was literally eating herself up with rage.

Such physical manifestations of long-simmering rage are quite common. Some extremely angry people develop ulcers; others suffer serious physical disorders. If you realize that you're hurting yourself as a result of unresolved anger, you should talk to a friend or a therapist. Even if your anger is justified, constant, unremitting anger is an extremely unhealthy sign. Anger should not be denied or repressed, of course; it should be dealt with and resolved.

Find your own way to get rid of anger. Here are some suggestions:

- Invent a ritual. Light a candle, or burn a photograph, or write your ex's name on a piece of paper, then tear it up and throw it down the toilet.

- Recall as many hurtful memories as you can, then write them in a journal—but don't reread them. When you get everything down on paper, throw the journal away.

- Talk your angry feelings into a tape recorder and don't censor yourself in any way. If it helps, punch a pillow as you do this.

- Yell out loud in the woods or at the beach. While you're at it, figuratively bury your ex under a tree or throw him into the ocean.

- Make a resolution that you're not going to let your ex have the power over you to make you so mad.

■ Promise yourself you'll get the best kind of revenge—that of suc-ceeding.

■ Volunteer to join an organization that helps women; channel your energies into improving the court system or combating such things as domestic violence.

When fathers are remiss about meeting their responsibilities, it may be because they're removed from the everyday lives of their children. Your anger will only push your ex-husband further from the day-to-day reality of family life. Controlling your anger may be hard, but it's best to find some constructive way to channel your emotions, one that won't com-pletely polarize your relationship with your former spouse.

Can Money Buy Kids' Love?

The other end of the ex-husband's financial spectrum can be a problem, too. Many dads make a point of showering their kids with gifts, taking them on fantastic vacations, and regularly treating them to the fast-food of their choice. This is nice, at first, but eventually a pattern emerges in which Disneyland Dad is the person the kids have fun with, while Mom is the one who handles all the drudge work and must instill discipline at home. You may feel some strong emotions if you find yourself in this situ-ation. Ask yourself if the ability to enjoy time with your children is really the kind of "competition" worth arguing over.

Sharon found herself resenting her ex-husband when the children would come home from visits with their father wearing new clothes and playing with expensive new toys. She felt that her ex was trying to show her up as being too cheap and too strict. When she reflected on this situation, though, she had to admit that when her ex bought clothes for the kids, she didn't have to spend her time, money, or energy doing so. She also realized that feeding anger into the situation only reinforced the "strict mom" stereo-type she was trying to avoid. Furthermore, she discovered that inquisitions served only to encourage her kids to feel guilty, or to downplay Dad's gen-erosity by "forgetting" to mention gifts and treats. Eventually, Sharon learned to let go of her anger.

The Long-Term Relationship— After the Relationship Ends

If you and your ex-spouse are in a situation where long-term financial help is part of the picture, it is in your interests to develop a stable, relatively conflict-free relationship, even though this may be difficult to do at first. A relationship marked by constant bitterness and antagonism will probably end up costing you money that you cannot afford to do without. If there are children in the relationship, the luxury of "getting things off your chest" on a regular basis may cause your kids to develop some unhealthy attitudes about adult relationships.

Many women make the mistake of thinking that once a divorce proceeding is concluded, one's relationship with an ex-husband comes to an end. In many cases—and certainly in the vast majority of cases where children are part of the equation—this is simply not true. The relationship has changed profoundly, but it still exists. Don't make the mistake of assuming you can turn your former mate into an enemy and, at the same time, expect a steady stream of financial help. Develop a working relationship, and try to keep crises to a minimum. In time, you will discover that this becomes a new relationship, one that features different objectives, but that may end up working with greater satisfaction for both parties.

Chapter 15

On the Job: Getting What You Deserve

*R*honda's boss gave her plenty of attention. He was very considerate, and, unlike many supervisors, he knew the importance
of compliment and public praise. He always thanked her profusely for
her help, and he made a habit of asking her for her opinions on important business decisions. Rhonda wanted to ask for a bigger raise than
her boss handed out every year, but she always decided not to—
because she felt that doing so would have been a betrayal somehow.
After all, she was the boss's favorite.

   Rhonda was seduced by her superior's easy camaraderie and constant attention. His care and concern, whether intended to do so or
not, had the effect of keeping her quiet. She craved the special attention she had earned from her boss—a kind of attention she had never
enjoyed while growing up—and she valued her situation too much to
threaten it by raising an issue as unpleasant as money.

Although you may not think that your outlook toward money—how you
feel about it and how comfortable you are discussing it—impacts your professional life, it does. Rhonda was unwilling to ask her boss for more money

because she felt that she would be betraying her boss's support by discussing this subject.

Your outlook on money affects how you behave and talk with your co-workers, the people who report to you, those outside your company with whom you do business, and ultimately, your boss.

Some people view a salary as a report card. They see the amount of money they make as an overall indicator of how they're doing in life. By this calculus, one's "worth" is measured in dollars and cents. The evidence is right there in black and white. If someone who does a similar job makes more money than you do, that can feel like you're "worth less" than you ought to be.

Is net worth the same thing as self-worth? No! It's important to keep your own sense of personal validity from becoming closely attached to the amount of money you earn. In this society, there tends to be a good deal of confusion about the two concepts, and that confusion can lead to some unfortunate situations. Don't be like the stockbroker whose libido turned out to be connected to the meanderings of the Dow-Jones Industrial Average. When the Dow was up, he had an active sex life, but when the indicator went down, he couldn't function as well! Such a state of affairs may seem amusing from a distance, but the all-too-common occurrence of having deep aspects of one's personal identity connected in an unhealthy way to one's earning patterns is anything but laughable.

You may or may not be what you eat, but you definitely *aren't* what you earn! If you find that your self-esteem is tied too closely to your attainments in the world of work and finance, you should use some of the exercises that appear elsewhere in this book to develop a better appreciation of your unique capacities as a person worthy of self-love.

There is a myth out there that some rational system is used by employers to determine what people ought to be paid. In more and more workplaces these days, there isn't.

Seniority used to play a much greater role than it now does in determining pay levels. These days, many companies have adopted scales that can seem (and often are) downright arbitrary. *Working Woman* magazine offers annual summaries on typical salaries for women in various jobs. If you're evaluating your own situation or contemplating a new job, you may find these articles to be helpful. Check your local library. Bear in mind, though, that compensation packages can vary dramatically depending on the area of the country where you live, the size and recent history of the employer, and "intangibles" such as whether or not the person hiring you graduated from the same school you did.

There's a paradox at work here. Even as women have begun to understand that their earnings are not a reflection of their value as people, many have also begun to feel, with some justification, that they have been taken advantage of when it comes to compensation, and that some changes are in order.

In large measure, this cycle arises from a conception of money as a taboo subject. Money is part of the "dirt" of the world, something one avoids talking about because it simply isn't "nice." This reluctance to discuss financial issues often leaves women in the position of being under-rewarded for the work they perform. When this is indeed the case, it's completely appropriate to take action.

Attention is nice. But it's no substitute for fairness.

People like Rhonda should take a long, hard look at the ways they have learned to think about their own compensation. It is certainly true that salary is not a meaningful indicator of our fundamental worth as human beings. It's also true, however, that by failing to discuss an issue of immediate importance to us simply because it involves money, we—the Rhondas of the world—run the very risk of being underpaid.

In order to broach the issue of fair compensation in a constructive way, people like Rhonda will have to learn to override their own "money-isn't-nice" attitude. They may also need to do a little inspired detective work. Determining what represents equitable pay can be a tricky business because organizations often cover up inconsistencies in employee salaries by doing their best to keep those salaries secret.

It's been said that many women are paid less than men because they don't place sufficient value on their own time. As a result, they charge less than men. There is certainly something to be said for this argument, but it doesn't really go as far as it should. Women often underprice themselves because they're raised to cultivate personal values of community, mutuality, personal sacrifice, and service—rather than the more competitive and hierarchical reward mindsets that are associated with cold, hard cash. Once they realize that these "communitarian" instincts are inherently positive workplace traits, they can assign a more realistic cash value to their services.

Salary Snooping

The secrecy that surrounds employee pay may be symbolized by the sealed envelope that the paycheck comes in, but with the right strategies, you can educate yourself enough to determine whether or not you should ask for more money. Here are some strategies to consider in that regard.

- **Take the direct approach.** Ask other people what they make. If you explain your situation sensitively and conclude by detailing your own salary, and if you explain to your coworker or colleague why you feel you have a good reason to know this information, most people will respond. Some will consider your request quite a compliment. Even people who may be uncomfortable stating their salary may be more than happy to let you know that your suspicions are correct, and that you are, in fact, being underpaid for what you do.

- **Be discreet and trustworthy.** When you talk about salaries, be sure you do it in a place that is private. Be sure to come across as asking for help, not demanding information. Reassure your colleague that you will maintain his or her confidentiality. That means that you won't write anything down, nor will you complain to your boss that you earn less than so-and-so.

- **Talk with someone who was hired very recently.** Believe it or not, the most recent employee hired often makes as much as 30 percent more money than a worker who has been doing the same or similar work at a high level of proficiency for several years. New people want to take jobs with a higher salary than they had at their old job, and hiring managers often feel they have to pay this to get them on board. Cost-of-living raises don't add up to much for employees who stay in one place.

- **Hit the library.** Ask to see the above-referenced *Working Woman* salary surveys—and then keep digging. Your trade association, whose periodicals are probably on file at the main branch of your local library, is a likely source of some of the most important statistics. The local Sunday paper's classified section can also be a helpful source of recent salary information in your region; check out the past month or two's editions. A friendly librarian can also point you toward the directories and government publications that document job classifications.

- **Work the phones.** Representatives of employment agencies and headhunting firms are valuable resources. Call them. Ask about the common salary ranges applicable to your industry and position, and be sure to take into account any regional cost-of-living factors that are applicable. Take into account, for instance, the fact that a legal secretary working in New York City is likely to earn more than one who performs similar tasks in Boise, Idaho.

Armed with the facts about how your current salary stacks up against the pay others in similar functions receive, you can now prepare your case. Take the time to write down why your performance should qualify you for a higher rung on the salary level. Develop several drafts before you attempt to discuss the matter with your supervisor, even on an informal basis.

By developing and reviewing a written brief, you'll be able to take steps toward overcoming the often extreme difficulty many women have in verbalizing their own achievements.

Sandra

"It's like bragging and being self-centered," lamented Sandra. "I was taught by my mother to do what I had to and not make a fuss in the process." As a result of years of such thinking, Sandra learned to take for granted her talents, her accomplishments, and her many contributions to the organization that employed her.

Not many of us get medals for doing something outstanding, so passing one along on our own initiative is sometimes in order. Recognizing our own fine points—on paper—is the next best thing to that kind of reward. Often, this exercise is a necessary counterbalance to years of neglect of the vital art of self-reinforcement.

When I asked Sandra what she thought she could do well on a professional level, she hemmed and hawed and was not able to come up with much of an answer. I asked her to tell me about her previous week at work. As she did so, it became obvious that she could envision a complex project from start to finish. She had the foresight to know how to execute tasks efficiently and head off potentially devastating problems before they developed. She knew how to talk to the people she supervised in a way that allowed them to improve their work without feeling criticized.

Sandra saw these accomplishments and talents as "just doing her job" until she realized—with a little coaching from me—that many of the contributions we reviewed together could have come from no one else in the organization.

What are your skills and natural talents? What do you bring to a job that's different or better than the things other people offer? Take some time and think of contributions you've made to your employer that were above and beyond the call of duty. Think of what would have happened if you had refused to contribute in the way you did, or if you'd been sick for a long period of time. Develop personal success anecdotes from the answers to the questions you ask yourself in these areas.

Once you are familiar with all the details of such stories, you should let your boss know how hard you work—regularly—not just at annual review time. Make a habit of submitting some kind of written progress report. When you work over the weekend, mention this in passing, and let your supervisor know how your contribution will not only make the company look good, but will also help improve her image within the organization.

When the time comes to ask for a raise, you'll be perfectly positioned to do so. Your request won't seem to be coming "out of the blue." In fact, because you've been dropping so many hints, your boss may well have been considering the raise issue already!

Common Attitudes

There are some common attitudes associated with asking for a raise that you may need to overcome.

PROCRASTINATION

This is usually a fear of something. Ask yourself what you're worried about. Could it be change, the unknown, or some other vague worry? Think of what you're worried about. Address your concerns to yourself before talking to your boss.

SELF-CRITICISM

We talk to strangers better and with more compassion than we do to ourselves. Just when you need support, you can hurt yourself by going into your self-doubt, self-critical mode. This is a bad habit, and the good news is that bad habits can be corrected in about five weeks. Behavioral therapists have helped people change the way that they talk to themselves by recommending that they wear a rubber band on their wrist and snap it when they find themselves thinking self-critically. The snap hurts just enough to get yourself to come up with a nicer way of talking to yourself. I call that tiny voice "the enemy." It's the voice from childhood that keeps us from enjoying ourselves, trying new things, and other life-enhancing things. part of everybody's therapy is to discipline that enemy. If you don't have someone to talk to about your own "voice" that says rotten things to you, try the rubber band.

PERFECTIONISM

This can keep a job search and everything else from happening. "If it's not done right, why do it?" was maybe your nagging thought. "I have to be 100% ready, and then I can proceed," you may say. Well, what if you do it in a "good enough" way? At least you started. Perfection doesn't exist. Do you want to try for something that you will always find fault with since you can't achieve it? I prefer the attitude of, "I'll see what I can do in the time allowed." When you work full-time, commute, come home late, tired, and hungry, you're just not going to be able to compose passionate or clever cover letters. So, conditions may never be perfect for the job of changing jobs. Are you willing to get up an hour earlier to do it? Can you find a "safe" public telephone near your office for your calls? Even if it's noisy, it's better than talking in the office where you might be uptight about being overheard.

Making the Request

Timing is everything when it comes to asking for a raise. If things are not quite right in the office because of such issues as low morale or an upcoming relocation, you should wait until things calm down to make your request. If your boss is having fits because of some personal problem or a budget deadline, put discussions of salary increases on hold. When is the best time to ask for a raise? When all systems are go—you've just done a great job on a project, profits are up, and your boss is centered, attentive, and willing to listen.

Always ask for more than you think you'll get. Bosses like to feel they're winning during these exchanges, so leave room for negotiation. You just might get the 15 percent increase you wanted if you ask for 25 percent—but your boss will think she saved a lot of money by negotiating you down. Let both parties claim a victory.

To bolster your case, bring in all the written evidence you've gathered or written that relates to your many sterling contributions. Letters from appreciative clients, memos recognizing your efforts to improve your own performance, bottom-line proof of how much money you saved or brought into the company—all these are powerful messages that you should pass along in black and white now. If you can demonstrate, on paper and in a compelling way, that you've made improvements in the way business is done or solved some thorny problem, you'll probably score points.

Here are some additional strategies to consider before you ask your boss for a raise.

- Visualize the scene. See yourself as prepared and confident. Play the scene out in your mind, complete with your boss's enthusiastic assent to your request.

- Prepare a list of the issues you want to discuss. If you can, highlight contributions you have made that are well beyond the scope of your formal job description. If there are budget hurdles that prevent you from winning greater compensation within the confines of your current position, consider asking for a new title. Many supervisors will respond quite well to this suggestion.

- Look your boss in the eye when you make your request, and don't smile as you talk.

- Consider asking a friend or colleague from work to do some role-playing exercises with you. Make the session as tough as possible. The better you prepare for the one-on-one session, the more likely it is to yield a positive outcome.

Asking for a raise—whether you do so on your own initiative or as part of the annual salary review process—means being assertive. Embrace that fact!

You can and should be assertive when it comes to negotiating a fair, realistic salary package for yourself, and you can do so without making the mistake of confusing your level of pay for your own validity as a person.

Stay reserved, calm, and professional throughout the discussion. Don't get emotional; remember that threatening to leave your present position if you don't get what you want is a strategy that usually backfires. Cite your research. Appeal to industry standards.

State what you think the situation is. State what you want. Attempt to arrive at a solution. In the process, get the other person's reaction and clarify key points. Be the adult, mature woman you are. Accept that it may take a while for your boss to get back to you with her response.

If the process doesn't result in the dollar increase you're after then consider other types of *non-monetary compensation.*

Ask About Non-Monetary Compensation

If you can't get an increase in salary, there's nothing wrong with asking for some additional perks. Consider finding out whether your employer will pick up the tab for a continuing education course, so you can learn more about spreadsheets or business letter writing. (You'll also be more marketable to another company after you take the courses, but don't bring that part up!) Other perks you should consider asking for include:

Extra vacation days

Child-care compensation

Bonus or stock options

Membership in professional associations or clubs

A company car or assistance with commuting expenses

Relying on Yourself, Reaching Out to Others for Help

In this book, you've learned about dozens of different strategies you can use when it comes to dealing intelligently with the financial issues that affect your relationships with the most important people in your life. You've also learned various strategies for making intelligent, mature choices about your own money—choices that place a premium on self-reliance, self-confidence, and a strong sense of who you are.

Before you finish this book, however, it's important to note that the suggestions you've read about between these covers are not a replacement for a relationship with a professional therapist or a qualified financial advisor. If you find that your situation warrants developing a relationship with one or both of these professionals, you should do so.

Observations on Working with a Therapist

A therapist should be a good listener and attentive to your needs. He or she should ask questions about your style, what you've tried before to change, and what worked and what didn't work. You want to feel comfortable talking with the therapist and you also want to check out his or her credentials.

Working with a Financial Advisor

You should not expect a financial advisor to

1. Educate you beyond an elementary level.

2. Shower you with attention or make you feel special beyond reasonable personal service.

3. Accept abuse for the risk or lack of return in any particular investment

If you decide to establish a relationship with a financial professional, do so for the right reasons. Good financial advisors are expert listeners—not unlike good therapists and counselors. They will look for the best ways to custom-fit your investments to your situation and your personality. Your advisor should gather information and outline all your options. Expecting more than that is likely to lead to an unhappy experience for you both.

One of the best ways to tell whether or not you've found a responsible financial professional is to listen for the questions that come your way. Is the person more interested in trying to sell you something, or learning more about your situation? Most clients are vague about goals. A trained professional will ask intelligent questions that will cast light on your feelings, desires, and underlying objectives. If the financial counselor you are meeting with doesn't want to know about your prior savings and investing experiences, and doesn't ask you questions that highlight short-term and long-term goals, there's almost certainly a problem somewhere.

The main reason you are sitting down with a financial advisor, of course, is to take advantage of his or her experience and knowledge. That may seem self-evident, but there are many stories of people who pay for the privilege of ignoring sound financial advice, and are simply interested in obtaining "cover" for indulging their own plans.

One of the best ways to find an advisor is to ask friends or other professionals such as attorneys or accountants to recommend one. Just as you would select a doctor carefully, you should talk to two or three financial advisors to see whether you feel comfortable with any of them.

If you would rather find someone on your own, you can get referrals from the professional associations:

International Association for Financial Planning
(800)945-4237

Institute of Certified Financial Planners
(800)322-4237

National Association of Personal Financial
Advisors (800)366-2732

I hope that by reading this book, you have been able to identify some of your own dominant financial patterns. Once you take the step of sitting down with a financial advisor, be sure to listen with an open mind to the advice you receive, even if that advice runs counter to your dominant money habit. Your financial advisor may be attempting to correct a long-standing strategy problem that is preventing you from attaining important objectives!

If you are a Keeper, be willing to look beyond your desire for security. Accumulating funds for their own sake may have pointed you toward a "no-risk" strategy that doesn't deliver the return you will need to meet key goals. You may want to discuss appropriate mutual funds with your financial advisor. Evaluate the risk inherent in each fund objectively, without rejecting it out of hand. Other people are getting good returns from shrewdly selected funds—why not you? Remember that risk is not an evil unto itself. Every investment carries some type of risk.

If you are a Love Buyer, make an effort to work with your financial advisor on prioritizing purchases and establishing a savings routine. You may know intellectually that some money categories are more important than others, but in any event, you may be sorely tempted to use money you should be committing to your savings on "impulse" purchases. Your financial advisor can probably help you set up an automatic savings plan that will place money directly into your IRA or other "off-limits" accounts.

If you are a Power Seeker, make an effort to show some flexibility, and recognize that following good advice is often incompatible with being the one who gives the orders. Taking risks and "thinking big" are sometimes, but not always, fine strategies. Think long and hard when assessing high-risk opportunities, and consider a second opinion before jumping in.

If you are a Freedom Searcher, it's a good bet that any kind of planning may rub you the wrong way. You may prefer instead to focus on the "now," the "today" aspects of life. You may need to develop a sound relationship with a financial planner more than any of the other members of the groups! Think of your contacts with this person as a direct, spontaneous way to deal with important financial issues and then move on to something else. For you, taking the first step of actually meeting with a financial advisor is the most important.

Once you start making intelligent financial decisions with your advisor's help, you'll gain confidence and a sense of mastery over financial issues that may have previously been intimidating to you. As it generally does when you tackle something new and come out smarter, your stock in yourself will go up. That's a "personal investment" goal that's always worth pursuing.

Good luck!

Bibliography

Altfest, Lewis J. and Karen Kaplan Altfest. *Lew Altfest Answers Almost All Your Questions about Money*. New York: McGraw-Hill, 1992.

Anthony, Joseph. "Thy Will Be Done." *Parenting* (May 1991): 25.

Barbanel, Linda. "Children and Money." *ParentGuide News* (December 1986): 10.

———. "Delicate Touch." *Registered Representative* (January 1991): 41.

———. *Fifty Favorite Questions about Kids and Money*. New York: Linda Barbanel, 1989.

———. "Giving a Child an Allowance: Learning Money Lessons—and More." *The Big Apple Parents' Paper* (September 1988): 18.

———. "Have You Got What it Takes to Be a Millionaire?" *Star* (17 January 1989).

———. "How to Handle Money." *ParentGuide News* (December 1988): 20.

———. "Know the Face and Feelings to Fit the Plan." *American Banker* (17 September 1984).

———. "Money Talk." *Bridal Guide* (November-December 1991): 33.

———. "Personality Behind the Portfolio." *The New York Times* Financial Planning Guide (19 May 1985).

———. *Piggy Bank to Credit Card*. New York: Crown, 1994.

———. "Piggy Bank Savvy." *Essence* (May 1986): 16.

————. "Women, Men . . . and Money." *Bridal Guide* (May-June 1991): 158.

————. "Why Do Women Sew Their Pockets Shut?" *The Executive Female* (March-April 1986).

Barber, Judy. "Communication Essential for Blended Families." *Family Money* (Summer 1995).

————. "It's Tough to Talk about Money and Mortality." *Family Money* (Summer 1993).

————. "Is It Good for Your Children?" *Family Money* (Fall 1995).

————. "Surviving Prenuptial Agreements." *Family Money* (Winter 1995).

Belsky, Gary and Beth Kobliner. "He Says She Says." *Money* (November 1993): p.77.

Berg, Adriane G. *How to Stop Fighting about Money & Make Some.* New York: Avon Books, 1988.

Bergler, Edmund. *Money and Emotional Conflicts.* New York: IUP, 1970.

Boundy, Donna. *When Money Is the Drug.* San Francisco: HarperSanFrancisco, 1993.

Damon, Janet. *Shopaholics.* New York: Avon Books, 1988.

Dobrzynski, Judith H. "How to Succeed? Go to Wellesley." *The New York Times* (Section 3): 1.

Dowling, Colette. *The Cinderella Complex.* New York: Summit Books, 1981.

Dunnan, Nancy. "A Few Words on Trading Places." *Lear's* (September 1990): 32.

Estess, Patricia Schiff. "When to Say 'Yes' & How to Say 'No.'" *Parade Magazine* (24 July 1988): 4.

Felton-Collins, Victoria and Suzanne Blair Brown. *Couples & Money*. New York: Bantam Books, 1990.

Forward, Susan and Craig Buck. *Money Demons*. New York: Bantam Books, 1994.

Goldberg, Herb and Robert Lewis. *Money Madness*. New York: New American Library, 1978.

Green, Michelle. "Control Freaks." *Self* (July 1992): 116.

Grodsky, Phyllis and Arthur Weinberger. "Apartners." *New York* (13 December 1982): 65.

Hansen, Joseph, Evelyn Reed, and Mary-Alice Waters. *Cosmetics, Fashions, and the Exploitation of Women*. New York: Pathfinder, 1986.

Henderson, Jim. "Winning Is the Easiest Part." *USA Today* (1 May 1989): 7B.

Jacoby, Susan. "The Balance of Power." *New Woman* (May 1992): 68.

———. "Cheapskates!" *Glamour* (May 1995): 272.

———. "Compulsive Shopping." *Glamour* (April 1986): 318.

———. "Envy." *Cosmopolitan* (December 1991): 163.

———. "Multiple Faces of Guilt." *Cosmopolitan* (1992): 148.

———. "People Who Can't Take." *Glamour* (December 1993): 229.

———. "Talking $$$ with Kids." *Family Circle* (October 1989): 47.

Janeway, Elizabeth. *Between Myth and Morning*. New York: William Morrow & Company, Inc., 1974.

Katz, Donald. "Men, Women & Money." *Worth* (June 1993): 56.

Lieberman, Annette and Vicki Lindner. *Unbalanced Accounts*. New York: The Atlantic Monthly Press, 1987.

Matthews, Arlene Modica. *Your Money, Your Self.* New York: Fireside, 1991.

McDonnell, Sharon. "Measuring Your Inner Resources." *Daily News* (28 January 1996).

McGoldrick, Monica and Randy Gerson. *Genograms in Family Assessment.* New York: W.W. Norton & Company, 1985.

McKay, Matthew, Patrick Fanning, and Kim Paleg. *Couple Skills*. Oakland: New Harbinger Publications, Inc., 1994.

Mellan, Olivia. *Money Harmony*. New York: Walker and Company, 1994.

Mogil, Christopher and Anne Stepian. "Money Between Friends." *More Than Money* (Summer 1993).

———. "Money and Couples." *More Than Money* (Autumn 1994).

———. "What Makes Giving Satisfying?" *More Than Money* (Autumn 1993).

———. " Money, Work, and Self-Esteem." *More Than Money* (Winter-Spring 1994).

Morris, Betsy. "Midlife Crisis." *Fortune* (18 September 1995): 60.

NAFE's Get-Ahead Guide #1. "How to Get a Raise." National Association for Female Executives, 1987.

Napolitane, Catherine and Victoria Pellegrino, Victoria. *Living & Loving after Divorce*. New York: Signet, 1977.

Oscar, Amy. "The Money Wars." *Parents* (October 1995): 112.

Pike, Elizabeth. "Tackling Sell Signs." *Personal Investor* (July 1989): 48–50.

Poduska, Bernard E. *For Love & Money*. Pacific Grove: Brooks/Cole, 1993.

Rowland, Mary. "Excess Baggage." *Worth* (November 1993): 120.

Sandroff, Ronni. "When Women Make More than Men." *Working Woman* (January 1994): 40.

Steinem, Gloria. *Moving Beyond Words*. New York: Simon & Schuster, 1994.

Weil, Anita. "The (Dangerously) Extravagant Man." *Cosmopolitan* (July 1995): 88.

Weinstein, Grace W. *Men, Women & Money*. New York: Signet, 1986.

White, Shelby. *What Every Woman Should Know about Her Husband's Money*. New York: Turtle Bay Books, 1992.

Willis, Clint. "The 5 Most Expensive Mistakes Women Make." *Working Woman* (September 1995): 42.

Yazigi, Monique. "Marrying Well." *The New York Times*, 5 November 1995): 13.l.

RECOMMENDED READING

Assets
Executive Female
Forbes
Fortune
Kiplinger's Personal Finance Magazine
Money
Smart Money
Working Mother
Worth

Index